THE LANGUAGE GYM
GRAMMAR BOOKLET I

THE LANGUAGE GYM
GRAMMAR BOOKLET I

FRENCH
SENTENCE BUILDERS
TRILOGY
PART I

A lexicogrammar approach
Beginner to Pre-Intermediate

GRAMMAR BOOK

About the authors

Gianfranco Conti taught for 25 years at schools in Italy, the UK and in Kuala Lumpur, Malaysia. He has also been a university lecturer, holds a Master's degree in Applied Linguistics and a PhD in metacognitive strategies as applied to second language writing. He is now an author, a popular independent educational consultant and professional development provider. He has written around 2,000 resources for the TES website, which have awarded him the Best Resources Contributor in 2015. He has co-authored the best-selling and influential book for world languages teachers, "The Language Teacher Toolkit" and "Breaking the sound barrier: Teaching learners how to listen", in which he puts forth his Listening As Modelling methodology. Gianfranco writes an influential blog on second language acquisition called The Language Gym, co-founded the interactive website language-gym.com and the Facebook professional group Global Innovative Language Teachers (GILT). He is also the founder and owner of the popular website, www.language-gym.com and, last but not least, Gianfranco has created the instructional approach known as **EPI** (Extensive Processing Instruction).

Dylan Viñales has taught for 15 years, in schools in Bath, Beijing and Kuala Lumpur in state, independent and international settings. He lives in Kuala Lumpur. He is fluent in five languages, and gets by in several more. Dylan is, besides a teacher, a professional development provider, specialising in **EPI**, metacognition, teaching languages through music (especially ukulele) and cognitive science. In the last five years, together with Dr Conti, he has driven the implementation of **EPI** in one of the top international schools in the world: Garden International School. This has allowed him to test, on a daily basis, the sequences and activities included in this book with excellent results (his students have won language competitions both locally and internationally). He has designed an original Spanish curriculum, bespoke instructional materials, based on Reading and Listening as Modelling (RAM and LAM). Dylan co-founded the fastest growing professional development group for modern languages teachers on Facebook, Global Innovative Languages Teachers, which includes over 12,000 teachers from all corners of the globe. He authors an influential blog on modern language pedagogy in which he supports the teaching of languages through **EPI** Dylan is the lead author of Spanish content on the Language Gym website and oversees the technological development of the site.

Aurélie Lethuilier has taught for 24 years and has been at her current school for 22 years (18 years as Curriculum Leader for Modern Languages). She is very passionate about teaching and learning and loves creating resources that will get the best out of students. She has been using and testing the **EPI** approach for a few years now and has successfully implemented it amongst her dedicated team of amazing teachers, without whom this journey would not have been possible. Aurélie is a key member of the Language Gym French team and has previously co-authored volumes such as French Verb Pivots and Primary French Sentence Builders 1 & 2. She is also a trusted editor of all three volumes of the Sentence Builders – French TRILOGY series. Aurélie is also an IT whizz who co-created the first ever Sentence Builders **EPI** PPT series, together with Ryan Cockrell.

Acknowledgements

We would like to thank our editors, **Ryan Cockrell** and **Ronan Jezequel**, for their tireless work, proofreading, editing and advising on this book. They are talented, accomplished professionals who work at the highest possible level and add value at every stage of the process. Not only this, but they are also lovely, good-humoured colleagues who go above and beyond, and make the hours of collaborating a real pleasure.

Our sincere gratitude to our team of incredible educators who helped in checking all the units involved in the proofreading of this volume. In particular a shoutout to: **Lorène Martine Carver, Jérôme Nogues, Barry Agnew, Darren Lester, Victoria Harrison, Alison Savage, Sev Bouclier, & Dawn Michael.** It is thanks to your time, patience, professionalism and detailed feedback that we have been able to produce such a refined and highly accurate product.

Finally, our gratitude to the MFL Twitterati for their ongoing support of **EPI** and the **Sentence Builders** book series.

Merci à tous,
Gianfranco, Dylan & Aurélie

Dedication

For Catrina
-Gianfranco

For Ariella & Leonard
-Dylan

For Horatio
-Aurélie

Introduction

This book was conceived as a supplement to our **French Sentence Builders: Trilogy – Part I** book. It is divided into 15 units, with matching Sentence Builders from the main Trilogy book. Each of the units is based around one **Main Grammar Focus**, which is explained and then taught via an array of engaging Conti, EPI, vocab building, translation and writing tasks. There are also additional **Pop-up Grammar** sections to introduce and teach other grammatical points required throughout the book.

This grammar book has been carefully crafted based on the following research-informed principles:

- a grammar teaching sequence should not move to production until the knowledge of the target grammar is established receptively
- the transition from the receptive to productive processing of the target grammar should be gradual and seamless
- the target grammar should be practised with vocabulary that the learners are highly familiar with in order to minimize cognitive load
- language learners should only be taught grammar structures which are highly frequent, have high surrender value and that they are developmentally ready to learn
- in order to prevent forgetting, the target grammar must be recycled several times over the weeks and months after it was first taught
- interleaving practice with two or more structures is beneficial for retention
- grammar teaching should be as multimodal as possible
- the synergy of explicit and implicit instruction is more effective than either type of instruction on its own
- automatic/fluent retrieval is a must when it comes to the most important grammatical features

It should be noted that every grammatical structure in this book is included in the new GCSE specification.

If you are an EPI user:

You will employ this book in the Awareness and Expansion/Explanation phases of the MARSEARS cycle. In the Awareness phase, you will simply raise your students' awareness of which grammatical structure you want them to focus on throughout the ensuing instructional sequence; in the latter Expansion/Explanation phase you will engage in a full-blown explanation of the target structure and will use the activities to drill it in.

Do remember that in EPI, grammar should be taught through all four language skills, hence you will also have to embed listening activities (e.g. Partial dictations, Aural sentence puzzles, Spot the difference, Spot the error and correct, Guess the next word, One of three, Sorting tasks, Track the structure), examples of which you can find in Conti and Smith's (2019) book "Breaking the sound barrier: teaching learners how to listen".

If you are not an EPI user:

This book will be very useful as it provides plenty of engaging, meaningful and research-informed grammar learning tasks targeting very frequent and useful structures which consitute the fundamentals of French grammar and will prepare your students effectively for the new GCSE speicification.

We hope you and your students enjoy using this grammar workbook.

Gianfranco, Dylan & Aurélie

"

SENTENCE BUILDERS TRILOGY - PART 1
GRAMMAR BOOKLET
TABLE OF CONTENTS

	TERM 1		
	Unit title	**Main Grammar Focus**	
0	EPI REGISTER ROUTINE: Introducing oneself	To conjugate *être* in the present indicative	**1**
1	Talking about my age	To conjugate *avoir* in the present indicative	**12**
2	Saying when my birthday is	Review of *être* in the present indicative	**25**
3	Saying where I live and am from	To use *en, au, à la, aux* + noun	**35**
4	*Things I like/dislike: School subjects & teachers (Optional)	To conjugate ER verbs in the present indicative	**47**
5	Things I like/dislike: Free time activities	To use *adorer, aimer* and *détester* in the present indicative + infinitive	**58**
	TERM 2		
6	Talking about my family members and myself + age	Review of *être* + using possessive adjectives (*mon, ton, son*)	**71**
7	*Describing my hair and eyes (Optional)	Review of *avoir* + using adjectives in the plural form	**82**
8	Describing myself and another family member	Review of *être*, adjectival agreements, possessive adjectives, *s'entendre*	**95**
9	Comparing people's appearance and personality	To use comparatives (*plus...que, moins...que, aussi...que*)	**104**
10	Describing my teachers and saying why I like them	Review of *être*, adjectival agreements, *adorer, aimer*	**117**
11	Saying what I and others do in our free time - Aller / Faire / Jouer	To conjugate *jouer, aller* and *faire* in the present indicative	**126**
	TERM 3		
12	Talking about my daily routine / school day	To use reflexive verbs (*se lever, s'habiller...*) in the present indicative	**139**
13	Talking about weekend plans	To form and use the immediate future	**150**
14	Talking about food: likes, dislikes & reasons	To review conjugation of verbs like *aimer* + adjectival agreements (masc/fem/plural). Review of verb *être*.	**160**
15	My holiday plans: travel plans & activities	Review of immediate future + introduction to the conditional	**173**

TERM 1

Main grammar focus:

- To conjugate *être*

Pop-up grammar:

- To use adjectival agreement

Comment tu t'appelles? *What is your name?*	**Je m'appelle** *My name is*	**Charles** **Marie**
Comment ça va aujourd'hui? *How are you today?*	**Ça va bien, merci** *I am well, thanks*	
Comment vas-tu? *How are you?*	**Je vais assez bien. Et toi?** *I am quite well. And you?*	

					MASC	FEM
Bonjour *Hello* **Bonsoir** *Good evening* **Salut** *Hi* **Au revoir** *Goodbye* **Bonne nuit** *Good night* **De rien** *You're welcome* **Merci** *Thank you* **Enchanté(e)** *Nice to meet you* **D'accord** *OK*	**aujourd'hui** **ça va** *today I am* **je vais** *I am*	**très bien** *very well* **bien** *well* **comme-ci,** **comme-ça** *(feeling)* *so-so* **mal** *(feeling)* *bad* **très mal** *(feeling)* *very bad*	**mais** **je suis** *but I am* *(feeling)* **car je suis** *because I am* *(feeling)*	**assez** *quite* **très** *very* **un peu** *a bit*	**détendu** *relaxed* **en colère** *angry* **énervé** *annoyed* **fatigué** *tired* **heureux** *happy* **malade** *sick* **stressé** *stressed* **triste** *sad*	**détendue** **en colère** **énervée** **fatiguée** **heureuse** **malade** **stressée** **triste**

MAIN GRAMMAR FOCUS
ÊTRE (TO BE) & ADJECTIVES

The verb **être** in this unit is used to express how we are feeling. The first three parts which we will practise here are **suis**, **es** and **est**.

Je suis	*I am*
Tu es	*You are*
Il est	*He is*
Elle est	*She is*

1. Match up

Je suis détendue.	She is annoyed.
Tu es stressé.	I am sick.
Elle est énervée.	He is happy.
Il est heureux.	I am relaxed.
Tu es fatiguée.	You are stressed.
Je suis malade.	He is angry.
Il est en colère.	You are tired.

2. Complete with the missing letters

a. J _ s _ _ s énervé.   *I am annoyed.*

b. T _ _ s heureux.   *You are happy.*

c. _ l _ st détendu.   *He is relaxed.*

d. _ ll _ _ st triste.   *She is sad.*

e. I _ e _ _ malade.   *He is sick.*

f. _ e _ ui _ stressée.   *I am stressed.*

3. Complete with the missing forms of *être*

a. Je _________ très en colère.   *I am very angry.*

b. Ma mère _______ assez stressée.   *My mother is quite stressed.*

c. Mon frère _________ un peu fatigué.   *My brother is a bit tired.*

d. Mon frère aîné ________ très détendu.   *My older brother is very relaxed.*

e. Tu _______ très malade.   *You are very sick.*

f. Ma sœur _______ un peu triste.   *My sister is a bit sad.*

g. Mon oncle ______ énervé.   *My uncle is annoyed.*

h. Je _____ un peu heureuse.   *I am a bit happy.*

4. Break the flow

a. Jevaistrèsbiencarjesuisdétendue.

b. Çavabiencarjesuisheureux.

c. Monfrèreestassezénervé.

d. Mamèreestunpeustressée.

e. Masœuresttrèsencolère.

f. Mononcleestassezfatigué.

g. Tuesunpeutristeaujourd'hui.

h. Tuestrèsénervéetstressé.

5. Faulty translation: fix the English

a. Je suis fatiguée.   *She is tired.*

b. Tu es en colère.   *I am angry.*

c. Elle est détendue.   *He is relaxed.*

d. Il est énervé.   *He is happy.*

e. Tu es stressé.   *You are tired.*

f. Je suis triste.   *I am stressed.*

g. Il est heureux.   *She is happy.*

h. Elle est malade.   *He is sick.*

6. Choose the correct verb

a. Je **suis / est / es** triste.

b. Tu **est / suis / es** heureuse.

c. Il **es / est / suis** en colère.

d. Elle **suis / es / est** énervée.

e. Tu **es / suis / est** détendu.

f. Elle **suis / est / es** heureuse.

g. Je **es / suis / est** triste.

h. Il **est / es / suis** fatigué.

7. Translate into French

a. I am happy. (m)

b. You are sad.

c. He is stressed.

d. She is annoyed.

e. You are angry.

f. I am relaxed. (f)

g. She is tired.

h. He is sick.

8. Complete with the missing adjectives

a. Je suis (f) très _______________ .   *I am very tired.*

b. Ma mère est assez _______________ .   *My mother is quite relaxed.*

c. Mon frère est un peu _______________ .   *My brother is a bit angry.*

d. Mon frère aîné est très _______________ .   *My older brother is very happy.*

e. Tu es (f) très _______________ .   *You are very sad.*

f. Ma sœur est un peu _______________ .   *My sister is a bit stressed.*

g. Mon oncle est _______________ .   *My uncle is sick.*

h. Je suis (f) un peu _______________ .   *I am a bit annoyed.*

POP-UP GRAMMAR
ADJECTIVES

Adjectives are used to describe a noun. They usually go after the noun (there are some exceptions which we will look at in another unit).

If an adjective ends in an **-e** in the masculine form it remains the same in the feminine:

Il est triste.	*He is sad.*	**Elle est triste.**	*She is sad.*
Il est malade.	*He is sick.*	**Elle est malade.**	*She is sick.*

If the adjective ends with an **-i** or a **-u** in the masculine form, you will need to add an **-e** in the feminine form:

Il est joli.	*He is handsome.*	**Elle est jolie.**	*She is pretty.*
Il est détendu.	*He is relaxed.*	**Elle est détendue.**	*She is relaxed.*

If the adjective ends with an **-é** in the masculine form, you will need to add an extra **-e** in the feminine form:

Il est énervé.	*He is annoyed.*	**Elle est énervée.**	*She is annoyed.*

If the adjective ends with **-eux** in the masculine form, it will change to **-euse** in the feminine form:

Il est heureux.	*He is happy.*	**Elle est heureuse.**	*She is happy.*

9. Match up

détendue (f)	annoyed
triste	sick
énervé (m)	happy
heureuse (f)	relaxed
fatigué (m)	sad
malade	angry
en colère	tired

10. Slalom translation

Je	Tu	Mon frère	Ma sœur	Mon oncle	Elle
est	est	est	es	suis	est
détendue	en colère	énervé	fatiguée	heureux	stressée
et triste	et malade	et énervée	mais stressé	et fatigué	et heureuse

a. I am tired and sick.

b. My brother is annoyed and sad.

c. She is relaxed and happy.

d. You are happy but stressed.

e. My uncle is angry and tired.

f. My sister is stressed and annoyed.

11. Translate into English

a. Je suis un peu triste.

b. Tu es très stressée.

c. Ma mère est très malade.

d. Mon frère aîné est assez heureux.

e. Elle est très fatiguée.

f. Tu es assez énervé.

g. Ma sœur est en colère.

h. Je suis très détendue.

12. Spot and correct the errors

a. Ma mère es très fatiguée.

b. Mon oncle est un peu énervée.

c. Ma sœur es triste.

d. Je sus malade.

e. Tu est assez détendue.

f. Elle est très heureux.

g. Il est un peu stressée.

h. Je sui en colère.

13. Choose the correct answer

a. Je suis **énervée / détendue / malade**.   *I am relaxed.*

b. Tu es **triste / en colère / heureux**.   *You are happy.*

c. Mon frère est **stressé / malade / détendu**.   *My brother is stressed.*

d. Ma mère est **fatiguée / heureuse / stressée**.   *My mother is tired.*

e. Il est **détendu / triste / malade**.   *He is sick.*

f. Elle est **en colère / énervée / fatiguée**.   *She is annoyed.*

14. Arrange the words in the correct order.

a. est énervé Mon frère stressé et — *My brother is stressed and annoyed.*

b. très détendue Je suis et heureuse — *I am very relaxed and happy.*

c. fatiguée Ma sœur est très malade assez et — *My sister is quite tired and very sick.*

d. un peu triste Tu es et énervée — *You are a bit sad and annoyed.*

e. en colère très stressée Elle est assez et — *She is quite angry and very stressed.*

f. mais un peu détendu un peu stressé Il est — *He is a bit relaxed but a bit stressed.*

g. très malade Je suis et un peu tu es triste — *I am very sick and you are a bit sad.*

h. est assez Ma mère heureuse — *My mother is quite happy.*

---

15. Guided translation: complete the translation

a. Today, I am a bit sick. — Aujourd'hui, je __________ un peu malade.

b. Today, I am very relaxed. (f) — Aujourd'hui, je suis très ______________ .

c. Today, you are quite annoyed. (m) — Aujourd'hui, tu es assez ______________ .

d. Today, my brother is angry. — Aujourd'hui, mon frère _______ en colère.

e. Today, my sister is quite sad. — Aujourd'hui, ma sœur est _________ ______________ .

---

16. Tangled translation

a. Je suis très **happy**. (f)

b. **You are** un peu **sick**.

c. Ma mère **is** très **angry**.

d. Mon frère aîné **is** très **relaxed**.

e. **She is** assez **stressed**.

f. **You are** assez **happy**. (m)

g. Ma sœur **is annoyed**.

h. **I am** très **tired**. (m)

17. Translate into French

a. I am a bit sick.

b. You are very happy. (f)

c. My mother is very relaxed.

d. My older brother is quite angry.

e. She is very sad.

f. You are quite stressed. (m)

g. My sister is tired.

h. I am very annoyed. (m)

No Snakes No Ladders

START	
1	I am
2	You are
3	He is
4	She is
5	I am relaxed (f).
6	I am angry.
7	I am annoyed (m).
8	He is happy and relaxed.
9	You are relaxed and happy (f).
10	I am angry and stressed (m).
11	You are sad.
12	You are stressed (f).
13	She is sick.
14	He is happy.
15	I am tired (f).
16	My uncle (m) is angry and tired.
17	My mother is very angry.
18	My sister is annoyed.
19	He is quite tired and very stressed.
20	She is very relaxed and a bit tired.
21	You are very happy (m).
22	She is sick and sad.
23	I am a bit sick.
24	I am relaxed and happy (f).
25	You are quite annoyed (f) and he is relaxed.
26	You are relaxed (f) and she is sad.
27	I am very angry and you are happy (f).
28	I am sick and tired (m).
29	You are very tired (f).
30	My brother is annoyed and sad.
FINISH	

No Snakes No Ladders

	1 Je suis	**2** Tu es	**3** Il est	**4** Elle est	**5** Je suis détendue (f).	**6** Je suis en colère.	**7** Je suis énervé (m).
DÉPART							
15 Je suis fatiguée (f).	**14** Il est heureux.	**13** Elle est malade.	**12** Tu es stressée (f).	**11** Tu es triste.	**10** Je suis en colère et stressé (m).	**9** Tu es détendue et heureuse (f).	**8** Il est heureux et détendu.
16 Mon oncle (m) est en colère et fatigué.	**17** Ma mère est très en colère.	**18** Ma sœur est énervée.	**19** Il est assez fatigué et très stressé.	**20** Elle est très détendue et un peu fatiguée.	**21** Tu es très heureux. (m)	**22** Elle est malade et triste.	**23** Je suis un peu malade.
ARRIVÉE	**30** Mon frère est énervé et triste.	**29** Tu es très fatiguée (f).	**28** Je suis malade et fatigué (m).	**27** Je suis très en colère et tu es heureuse. (f)	**26** Tu es détendue (f) et elle est triste.	**25** Tu es assez énervée (f) et il est détendu.	**24** Je suis détendue et heureuse. (f)

UNIT 0 – FAST & FURIOUS – ROUND 1

1.   Bonjour. _____ _____ assez _____________.
Hello. I am quite relaxed.

2.   Salut. Tu es un peu ___________ mais ____________.
Hi. You are a bit tired but happy.

3.   Il est très _____ _________ et _________.
He is very angry and annoyed.

4.   _____ _____ un peu __________.
She is a bit sick.

5.   _____ _____ très _________ et _________.
I am very happy and relaxed.

	Time 1	**Time 2**	**Time 3**	**Time 4**
Time				
Mistakes				

UNIT 0 – FAST & FURIOUS – ROUND 2

1.   Bonjour. _____ _____ assez _____________.
Hello. I am quite sick.

2.   Salut. Tu es un peu ___________ mais ____________.
Hi. You are a bit sad but relaxed.

3.   Il est très _________ et _____ _________.
He is very stressed and angry.

4.   _____ _____ un peu __________.
She is a bit annoyed.

5.   _____ _____ très _________ et _________.
I am very tired and sick.

	Time 1	**Time 2**	**Time 3**	**Time 4**
Time				
Mistakes				

ASSESSMENT ROUND

1. Choose the correct translation (you won't need two of the sentences)

a. Je suis assez détendue mais je suis fatiguée. _____

b. Mon frère est un peu énervé et un peu en colère. _____

c. Ma mère est très en colère. _____

d. Tu es fatigué mais tu es heureux. _____

e. Ma sœur est malade et assez stressée. _____

    1.   My mother is very angry.
    2.   My mother is very annoyed.
    3.   I am quite relaxed but I am tired.
    4.   My sister is sick and quite stressed.
    5.   My brother is a bit annoyed and a bit tired.
    6.   You are tired but you are happy.
    7.   My brother is a bit annoyed and a bit angry.

2. Fill in the gaps with the missing words

a. Je _____________ très triste et un peu malade.

b. Ma sœur est un peu _____________.

c. Mon frère est en _____________ et très stressé.

d. Tu es assez _____________ et heureux.

e. Aujourd'hui tu _____________ assez énervée.

détendu	colère	suis	es	fatiguée

3. Translate the sentences into French

a. Today, I am very well but I am a bit tired. (m)

b. Today, I am well because I am happy. (f)

c. Today, he is (feeling) very sick.

d. Today, she is (feeling) a bit stressed.

e. Today, you are (feeling) quite relaxed. (f)

UNIT 1
Talking about my age

Main grammar focus:

- To conjugate *avoir* in the present indicative

Pop-up grammar:

- To conjugate *s'appeler*

UNIT 1
Talking about my age

Comment tu t'appelles? *What is your name?*	**Quel âge as-tu?** *How old are you?*
Comment s'appelle ton frère? *What is your brother's name?*	**Quel âge a-t-il?** *How old is he?*
Comment s'appelle ta sœur? *What is your sister's name?*	**Quel âge a-t-elle?** *How old is she?*

Je *I*	**m'appelle** *am called*			**j'ai** *I have**	**un** 1	**an** *year*
Mon frère *My brother* **Ma sœur** *My sister*	**s'appelle** *is called*	Alexandre Anthony Annabelle Béatrice Charles Denis Émilie Frédéric Isabelle Joséphine Julien Marie Paul Tristan	**et** *and*	**il/elle a** *he/she has**	deux 2 trois 3 quatre 4 cinq 5 six 6 sept 7 huit 8 neuf 9 dix 10 onze 11 douze 12 treize 13 quatorze 14 quinze 15	**ans** *years*
Author's note: in French we use the verb "avoir" [to have] to talk about age **although "J'ai quatre ans" literally means "I have four years", in English, it's translated as "I am four years old"*						

MAIN GRAMMAR FOCUS
AVOIR & ÂGE – TO BE & AGE

The verb **avoir** in this unit is used to express how old we are. **J'ai dix ans** would be literally translated as *I have ten years* (as in "I have been living for ten years").

The first three parts which we will practise here are **ai**, **as** and **a**.

J'ai	*I have*
Tu as	*You have*
Il a	*He has*
Elle a	*She has*

1. Match up	
J'ai quinze ans.	I am six.
Il a huit ans.	She is three.
J'ai six ans.	I am thirteen.
Tu as dix ans?	He is eight.
Elle a trois ans.	How old are you?
Quel âge as-tu?	Are you ten?
J'ai treize ans.	I am fifteen.

2. Complete with the missing letters

a. J'_ _ onze ans. *I am eleven.*

b. T _ _ s six ans. *You are six.*

c. _ l _ quatorze ans. *He is fourteen.*

d. _ ll _ _ treize ans. *She is thirteen.*

e. _ u a _ trois ans. *You are three.*

f. _ 'ai n _ _ f ans. *I am nine.*

THE LANGUAGE GYM
GRAMMAR BOOKLET I

3. Complete with the missing form of *avoir*

a. Salut! J'_______ sept ans.	*Hi! I am seven.*
b. Mon amie _______ quinze ans.	*My friend is fifteen.*
c. Mon frère _________ onze ans.	*My brother is eleven.*
d. Mon frère aîné _______ huit ans.	*My older brother is eight.*
e. Mon petit frère _______ neuf ans.	*My little brother is nine.*
f. Quel âge ____-tu?	*How old are you?*
g. J'_____ douze ans.	*I am twelve years old.*
h. Tu _____ dix ans.	*You are ten.*

4. Break the flow

a. Bonjour!Jaiquatorzeans.

b. Jaicinqans.

c. Ilaseptans.

d. Elleadouzeans.

e. Mapetitesœurahuitans.

f. Ilatreizeans.

g. Quelâgeastu?

h. Monfrèreaînéaonzeans.

5. Faulty translation: fix the English

a. J'ai six ans.	*I have six.*
b. Il a treize ans.	*She is thirteen.*
c. Elle a huit ans.	*She is nine.*
d. Il a quinze ans.	*He is fourteen.*
e. Tu as quatre ans.	*He is four.*
f. J'ai trois ans.	*You are three.*
g. Il a un an.	*She is one.*
h. Elle a sept ans.	*He is seven.*

6. Choose the correct verb

a. J' **ai** / **a** / **as** trois ans.

b. Tu **as** / **a** / **ai** quatorze ans.

c. Quel âge **ai** / **as** / **a** -tu?

d. Elle **a** / **ai** / **as** onze ans.

e. Tu **ai** / **as** / **a** neuf ans.

f. Elle **ai** / **a** / **as** quinze ans.

g. J' **a** / **ai** / **as** cinq ans.

h. Il **as** / **ai** / **a** un an.

7. Translate into French

a. I am twelve.

b. You are eight.

c. He is thirteen.

d. She is seven.

e. You are two.

f. I am three.

g. She is fourteen.

h. He is eleven.

POP-UP GRAMMAR
S'APPELER - TO BE CALLED

S'appeler is a reflexive verb and it means *To be called* as in *to call oneself*.

The first three parts which we will practise here are **m'appelle**, **t'appelles** and **s'appelle**.

Je m'appelle	*I am called / My name is*
Tu t'appelles	*You are called / Your name is*
Il s'appelle	*He is called / His name is*
Elle s'appelle	*She is called/ Her name is*

8. Match up

Je m'appelle Paul.	Your name is Joe.
Tu t'appelles Joe.	My name is Théo.
Elle s'appelle Lou.	Your name is Sam.
Il s'appelle Luc.	My name is Paul.
Je m'appelle Théo.	Her name is Lou.
Il s'appelle Nadim.	His name is Luc.
Tu t'appelles Sam.	His name is Nadim.

9. Complete with the missing form of *s'appeler* or the subject pronouns

a. Je _______________ Sandra.   *My name is Sandra.*

b. Ma mère _______________ Marie.   *My mother is called Marie.*

c. Mon frère _______________ Théo.   *My brother is called Théo.*

d. Mon frère aîné _______________ Antoine.   *My older brother is called Antoine.*

e. Comment tu _______________?   *What's your name?*

f. _____ m'appelle Jérôme.   *My name is Jérôme.*

g. _____ s'appelle Dylan.   *His name is Dylan.*

h. _____ t'appelles Gian.   *Your name is Gian.*

10. Slalom translation

Je	Mon frère	Ma sœur	Comment	Mon ami	Mon amie
s'appelle	tu	m'appelle	s'appelle	s'appelle	s'appelle
Tristan	Charles	t'appelles?	Denis	Marie	Béatrice
Quel âge	et j'ai	et il a	et elle a	et il a	et elle a
neuf ans	as-tu?	quatorze ans	douze ans	huit ans	quatre ans

a. My name is Denis and I am eight years old.

b. My brother is called Charles and he is fourteen years old.

c. My sister is called Béatrice and she is four years old.

d. What's your name? How old are you?

e. My friend is called Tristan and he is twelve years old.

f. My friend is called Marie and she is nine years old.

11. Translate into English

a. J'ai onze ans.

b. Elle s'appelle Annabelle.

c. Ma sœur a quinze ans.

d. Mon frère aîné a huit ans.

e. Elle a treize ans.

f. Quel âge a-t-il?

g. Comment s'appelle ton frère?

h. Comment tu t'appelles?

12. Spot and correct the errors

a. Ma mère appelle Joséphine.

b. Mon frère as quatorze ans.

c. Ma sœur ai dix ans.

d. Je suis onze ans.

e. Comment tu t'appelle?

f. Quel âge a elle?

g. Il est quatorze ans.

h. Je ai sept ans.

13. Choose the correct answer

a. **Elle s'appelle / Je m'appelle / Tu t'appelles** Laure.   *My name is Laure.*

b. Tu as **trois / treize / neuf** ans.   *You are nine years old.*

c. Mon frère a **douze / dix / deux** ans.   *My brother is twelve years old.*

d. Mon amie a **six / huit / onze** ans.   *My friend is eight years old.*

e. **Je m'appelle / Il s'appelle / Elle s'appelle** Lou.   *Her name is Lou.*

f. Ma sœur a **quinze / treize / dix** ans.   *My sister is fifteen years old.*

14. Arrange the words in the correct order.

a. Je Émilie m'appelle et douze j'ai ans   *My name is Émilie and I am twelve.*

b. Mon frère a ans quinze   *My brother is fifteen.*

c. Marie Ma sœur sept ans a   *My sister Marie is seven.*

d. t'appelles tu Comment?   *What's your name?*

e. Mon ami treize ans a   *My friend is thirteen.*

f. Mon Isabelle amie ans dix a   *My friend Isabelle is ten.*

g. Quel as-tu âge? huit J'ai ans   *How old are you? I am eight.*

h. Tu Anthony t'appelles et cinq ans tu as   *Your name is Anthony and you are five.*

15. Guided translation: complete the translation

a. Today, I am nine years old.   Aujourd'hui, j' ________ neuf ans.

b. She is five years old.   ________ ________ cinq ans.

c. My name is Suzanne.   ________ _______________ Suzanne.

d. My brother is called Pierre.   Mon frère ________________ Pierre.

e. What's your name?   Comment tu _________________?

f. How old are you?   ___________ _________ as-tu?

16. Tangled translation

a. J'ai onze **years old.**

b. **You have** huit ans.

c. Ma mère **has** quarante ans.

d. Mon frère aîné **is called** Denis.

e. **She has** six ans.

f. Comment **is your name?**

g. **How old** as-tu?

h. **What** s'appelle-t-elle?

17. Translate into French

a. What's your name?

b. My name is Claire.

c. How old are you?

d. I am twelve years old.

e. My sister is four years old.

f. What's her name?

g. My brother is three years old.

h. How old is he?

UNIT 1 – ORAL PING PONG – Person A

ENGLISH	FRENCH	ENGLISH	FRENCH
I am called Alexandre.	Je m'appelle Alexandre.	**What is your name?**	Comment tu t'appelles?
I am four.		**I am seven.**	
My brother is called Charles.	Mon frère s'appelle Charles.	**I am thirteen.**	J'ai treize ans.
How old are you?		**My brother is twelve.**	
My sister is eleven.	Ma sœur a onze ans.	**My brother is called Frédéric.**	Mon frère s'appelle Frédéric.
How old is he?		**My sister is fifteen.**	
My sister is called Isabelle.	Ma sœur s'appelle Isabelle.	**I am eleven.**	J'ai onze ans.
My brother is called Tristan.		**My name is Annabelle.**	
I am fourteen.	J'ai quatorze ans.	**My sister is two.**	Ma sœur a deux ans.
I am five.		**What is your sister's name?**	

UNIT 1 – ORAL PING PONG – Person B

ENGLISH	FRENCH	ENGLISH	FRENCH
I am called Alexandre.		What is your name?	
I am four.	J'ai quatre ans.	I am seven.	J'ai sept ans.
My brother is called Charles.		I am thirteen.	
How old are you?	Quel âge as-tu?	My brother is twelve.	Mon frère a douze ans.
My sister is eleven.		My brother is called Frédéric.	
How old is he?	Quel âge a-t-il?	My sister is fifteen.	Ma sœur a quinze ans.
My sister is called Isabelle.		I am eleven.	
My brother is called Tristan.	Mon frère s'appelle Tristan.	My name is Annabelle.	Je m'appelle Annabelle.
I am fourteen.		My sister is two.	
I am five.	J'ai cinq ans.	What is your sister's name?	Comment s'appelle ta sœur?

No Snakes No Ladders

	1	2	3	4	5	6	7
START	I have	You have	He has	She has	I am 7 years old.	You are 10 years old.	He is 12 years old.
15 His name is Charles and he is 15 years old.	**14** Your name is Pierre and you are 5 years old.	**13** My name is Claire and I am 9 years old.	**12** Her name is Isabelle.	**11** His name is Tristan.	**10** Your name is Annabelle.	**9** My name is Paul.	**8** She is 14 years old.
16 Her name is Béatrice and she is 13 years old.	**17** I am 11 years old.	**18** You are 4 years old.	**19** His name is Joseph.	**20** Her name is Suzanne.	**21** What's your name?	**22** What is your brother's name?	**23** What is your sister's name?
FINISH	**30** My brother is 12 years old.	**29** My sister is 3 years old.	**28** I am 15 years old.	**27** How are you?	**26** How old is she?	**25** How old is he?	**24** How old are you?

No Snakes No Ladders

	1	2	3	4	5	6	7
DÉPART	J'ai	Tu as	Il a	Elle a	J'ai sept ans.	Tu as dix ans.	Il a douze ans.
15 Il s'appelle Charles et il a quinze ans.	**14** Tu t'appelles Pierre et tu as cinq ans.	**13** Je m'appelle Claire et j'ai neuf ans.	**12** Elle s'appelle Isabelle.	**11** Il s'appelle Tristan.	**10** Tu t'appelles Annabelle.	**9** Je m'appelle Paul.	**8** Elle a quatorze ans.
16 Elle s'appelle Béatrice et elle a treize ans.	**17** J'ai onze ans.	**18** Tu as quatre ans.	**19** Il s'appelle Joseph.	**20** Elle s'appelle Suzanne.	**21** Comment tu t'appelles?	**22** Comment s'appelle ton frère?	**23** Comment s'appelle ta sœur?
ARRIVÉE	**30** Mon frère a douze ans.	**29** Ma sœur a trois ans.	**28** J'ai quinze ans.	**27** Comment vas-tu?	**26** Quel âge a-t-elle?	**25** Quel âge a-t-il?	**24** Quel âge as-tu?

UNIT 1 – FAST & FURIOUS – ROUND 1

1.   Bonjour. _____________ tu t' _____________?
Hello. What's your name?

2.   Salut. ___ _____________ Claire et _______ douze ans.
Hi. My name is Claire and I am twelve years old.

3.   Il est très _____________ et _____________.
He is very relaxed and happy.

4.   _____________ s'_____________-t-il?
What's his name?

5.   Ma sœur _____________ Émilie et ______ ___ treize ans.
My sister is called Émilie and she is thirteen years old.

	Time 1	Time 2	Time 3	Time 4
Time				
Mistakes				

UNIT 1 – FAST & FURIOUS – ROUND 2

1.   Bonjour. _____________ tu t' _____________?
Hello. What's your name?

2.   Salut. ___ _____________ Pierre et _______ onze ans.
Hi. My name is Pierre and I am eleven years old.

3.   Elle est très ___ _____________ et _____________.
He is very angry and stressed.

4.   _____________ s'_____________-t-elle?
What's her name?

5.   Ma sœur _____________ Annabelle et ______ ___ six ans.
My sister is called Annabelle and she is six years old.

	Time 1	Time 2	Time 3	Time 4
Time				
Mistakes				

ASSESSMENT ROUND

1. Choose the correct translation (you won't need two of the sentences)

a. Je suis assez fatiguée mais je suis heureuse.   _____

b. Mon frère s'appelle Paul et il a treize ans.   _____

c. Ma mère s'appelle Claire et elle a les yeux verts.   _____

d. Tu es fatigué mais tu es heureux.   _____

e. Ma sœur s'appelle Sandra et elle a dix ans.   _____

1. My sister is called Sandra and she is 11.
2. I am quite tired but I am happy.
3. My mother is called Claire and she has green eyes.
4. My sister is called Sandra and she is 10.
5. My brother is called Paul and he is 3.
6. You are tired but you are happy.
7. My brother is called Paul and he is 13.

2. Fill in the gaps with the missing words

a. Je suis très détendu mais un peu ______________ .

b. Ma sœur ______________ Joséphine.

c. J'______________ douze ans.

d. ______________ tu t'appelles?

e. Aujourd'hui tu ______ assez énervée.

s'appelle	malade	comment	es	ai

3. Translate the sentences into French

a. Today, I am very well but I am a bit tired. (m)

b. My name is Marie and I am* 11 years old.

c. Today, he is very happy.

d. What's your name?

e. His name is Anthony and he is* 8 years old.

Main grammar focus:

- Review of *être* in the present indicative

UNIT 2
Saying when my birthday is

				1 premier *first* 2 deux 3 trois 4 quatre 5 cinq 6 six 7 sept 8 huit 9 neuf 10 dix 11 onze 12 douze 13 treize	
Comment tu t'appelles? *What is your name?* **D'où es-tu?** *Where are you from?* **Quel âge as-tu?** *How old are you?* **Quelle est la date de ton anniversaire?** *When is your birthday?*			**Comment s'appelle ton ami(e)?** *What is your friend's name?* **D'où est-il/est-elle?** **Quel âge a-t-il/a-t-elle?** *How old is he/she?* **Quelle est la date de son anniversaire?** *When is his/her birthday?*		

Je m'appelle Julien *I am called Julien*	**je suis de Paris** *I am from Paris* ***j'ai X ans** *I am X years old*	**et** *and*	**mon anniversaire est le** *my birthday is the*	1 premier *first* 2 deux 3 trois 4 quatre 5 cinq 6 six 7 sept 8 huit 9 neuf 10 dix 11 onze 12 douze 13 treize 14 quatorze 15 quinze 16 seize 17 dix-sept 18 dix-huit 19 dix-neuf 20 vingt	**janvier** *January* **février** **mars** **avril** **mai** **juin** **juillet** **août** **septembre** **octobre** **novembre** **décembre**
Mon amie s'appelle Catherine *My friend is called Catherine* **Mon ami s'appelle Francis** *My friend is called Francis*	**il/elle est de Biarritz** *he/she is from Biarritz* ***il/elle a X ans** *he/she is X years old*		**son anniversaire est le** *his/her birthday is the*	21 vingt-et-un 22 vingt-deux 23 vingt-trois 24 vingt-quatre 25 vingt-cinq 26 vingt-six 27 vingt-sept 28 vingt-huit 29 vingt-neuf 30 trente 31 trente-et-un	

AUTHOR'S NOTE: *J'ai or il/elle a actually means "I have" and "he/she has" in French. You use this verb for telling age. You will see it many times throughout this booklet! ☺

MAIN GRAMMAR FOCUS
ÊTRE – TO BE

We can use the verb **être** to say where we are from and when our birthday is.

Je suis de France   *I am from France*

Mon anniversaire est le 31 août   *My birthday is on the 31st August*

Je suis	*I am*	**Nous sommes**	*We are*
Tu es	*You are*	**Vous êtes**	*You (guys) are*
Il est	*He is*	**Ils sont**	*They are*
Elle est	*She is*	**Elles sont**	*They are*

---

1. Match up

Tu es de Paris.	She is from Caen.
Je suis de Dijon.	He is from Dieppe.
Elle est de Caen.	They are from Rouen.
Il est de Dieppe.	You are from Paris.
Je suis d'Aix.	You (guys) are from Nice.
Ils sont de Rouen.	I am from Aix.
Vous êtes de Nice.	I am from Dijon.

2. Complete with the missing letters

a. Je s _ _ s de Brest.   *I am from Brest.*

b. T _ _ s de Caen.   *You are from Caen.*

c. _ l e _ _ de Nice.   *He is from Nice.*

d. El _ e _ st d'Aix.   *She is from Aix.*

e. Il _ s _ _ _ de Lille.   *They are from Lille.*

f. D'où _ _ -tu?   *Where are you from?*

g. _ _ es _ d _ Paris.   *He is from Paris.*

3. Complete with the missing form of "Être"

a. Je ___________ de Toulouse.

I am from Toulouse.

b. Mon anniversaire ___________ le deux juin.

My birthday is the 2nd June.

c. Nous ___________ de Bordeaux.

We are from Bordeaux.

d. Mon frère aîné ___________ de Paris.

My older brother is from Paris.

e. Elles ne ___________ pas de Nantes.

They are not from Nantes.

f. D'où _________-tu?

Where are you from?

g. Mon anniversaire ___________ le dix mars.

My birthday is on the 10th March.

h. D'où ___________-vous?

Where are you (guys) from?

4. Break the flow

a. Bonjour!JesuisdeLille.

b. Doùestu?

c. IlssontdeMarseille.

d. NoussommesdeLimoges.

e. MapetitesœurestdeCalais.

f. Monanniversaireestledouzemai.

g. Quelleestladatedetonanniversaire?

h. VousêtesdeMadrid.

5. Faulty translation: fix the English

a. D'où es-tu?   *Where do you live?*

b. Il est de Nantes.   *She is from Nantes.*

c. Elle est de Poitiers.   *He is from Poitiers.*

d. Tu es de Bruxelles.   *I am from Brussels.*

e. Ils sont de Nice.   *They are nice.*

f. Vous êtes de Tunis?   *You are from Tunis.*

g. Elle est de Paris.   *She lives in Paris.*

h. Il est de Toulouse.   *He went to Toulouse.*

6. Choose the correct verb

a. Je **suis / est / es** de Fécamp.

b. Tu **est / suis / es** de Casablanca.

c. Vous **êtes / est / suis** de Bruxelles.

d. Elle **suis / es / est** de Marrakech.

e. Tu **es / suis / est** de Lyon.

f. Elles **suis / sont / es** de Dieppe.

g. Je **es / suis / est** de Biarritz.

h. Nous **est / es / sommes** de Bordeaux.

7. Translate into French

a. I am from Strasbourg.

b. They (m) are from Dijon.

c. He is from Montpellier.

d. She is from Grenoble.

e. You (guys) are from Dakar.

f. We are from Montréal.

g. She is from Tahiti.

h. You are from Toulon.

8. Complete with the missing form of *avoir*, *être* or *s'appeler*

a. Comment tu t'_________?

What's your name?

b. Mon amie s'_________ Béatrice.

My friend is called Béatrice.

c. Je _________ de Bordeaux.

I am from Bordeaux.

d. Mon frère aîné _______ neuf ans.

My older brother is 9.

e. J'_________ douze ans.

I am 12.

f. Quel âge ____-tu?

How old are you?

g. Mon anniversaire _________ le vingt-huit avril.

My birthday is on the 28th April.

h. D'où _________-elle?

Where is she from?

9. Slalom translation

Je m'appelle	Je m'appelle	Mon	Mon amie	Mon ami	Son
Patrick	anniversaire	s'appelle	Isabelle	anniversaire	s'appelle
est le	Susie	et j'ai	Paul	et je suis	est le
et elle est	vingt-trois	premier	de	et il est	trente
de Bruxelles	de Dieppe	Caen	octobre	ans	août

a. My name is Isabelle and I am 23 years old.

b. My name is Patrick and I am from Caen.

c. My birthday is on the 1st October.

d. My friend is called Susie and she is from Dieppe.

e. My friend is called Paul and he is from Brussels.

f. Her birthday is on the 30th August.

10. Translate into English

a. Son anniversaire est le vingt-deux juin.

b. Mon ami s'appelle Marc.

c. J'ai quatorze ans.

d. Mon amie a dix-huit ans.

e. Nous sommes de Toulouse.

f. Comment s'appelle ton ami?

g. D'où êtes-vous?

h. Je suis de Rouen.

11. Spot and correct the errors

a. Mon anniversaire a le trois mai.

b. Mon ami s'appelle Isabelle.

c. Je sui de Calais.

d. D'ou es-tu?

e. Sont anniversaire est le quinze juillet.

f. Quelle a la date de son anniversaire?

g. Elle as trente ans.

h. Comment t'appelle ton amie?

12. Choose the correct answer	
a. D'où **es-tu?** / **est-il?** / **est-elle?**	*Where are you from?*
b. **Je m'appelle** / **Tu t'appelles** / **Elle s'appelle** Marie.	*Your name is Marie.*
c. **Nous sommes** / **Vous êtes** / **Ils sont** de Paris.	*You (guys) are from Paris.*
d. Son anniversaire est le premier **mai** / **juin** / **juillet**.	*Her birthday is the first June.*
e. J'ai **cinq** / **quinze** / **vingt-cinq** ans.	*I am fifteen.*
f. **Mon amie** / **Mon père** / **Ma mère** est de Quimper.	*My father is from Quimper.*

13. Arrange the words in the correct order.	
a. s'appelle Comment ton ami?	*What's your friend's name?*
b. Mon ami Damien s'appelle	*My friend is called Damien.*
c. de Il est Biarritz	*He is from Biarritz.*
d. vingt-et-un Il a ans	*He is 21 years old.*
e. Son est anniversaire février le vingt-sept	*His birthday is on the 27th February.*
f. es-tu D'où?	*Where are you from?*
g. ton anniversaire est la date Quelle de?	*When is your birthday?*
h. Carole Mon amie Nantes est de	*My friend Carole is from Nantes.*

14. Tangled translation
a. **I am*** vingt-huit ans.
b. **My friend is called** Anthony.
c. Son anniversaire **is** le vingt-trois juin.
d. **Where** est-il?
e. **When** est la date de ton **birthday**?
f. **They (f) are from** Rennes.
g. Mon ami **is*** trente-et-un ans.
h. **My birthday** est le quatre **July**.

15. Translate into French
a. My name is Tristan.
b. I am 16 years old.
c. I am from Casablanca.
d. My birthday is on the 25th December.
e. My friend is called Nathalie.
f. She is from Papeete.
g. What is your friend's name?
h. Where is he from?

No Snakes No Ladders

START	1 – I have	2 – I am from	3 – My name is	4 – He has	5 – He is from	6 – His name is	7 – She has
15 – My friend is called Jérôme.	14 – What is your friend's name?	13 – I am* 19.	12 – My birthday is the 5th November.	11 – I am from Alger.	10 – My name is Sophie.	9 – Her name is	8 – She is from
16 – Where is he from?	17 – He is from Toulouse.	18 – How old is he?	19 – He is* 30.	20 – When is your birthday?	21 – His birthday is on the 12th May.	22 – My friend is called Vanessa.	23 – How old is she?
FINISH	30 – I am from Tunis.	29 – Where are you from?	28 – Her birthday is on the 12th November.	27 – When is her birthday?	26 – She is from Paris.	25 – Where is she from?	24 – She is 31.

No Snakes No Ladders

	1 J'ai	2 Je suis de	3 Je m'appelle	4 Il a	5 Il est de	6 Il s'appelle	7 Elle a
DÉPART							
15 Mon ami s'appelle Jérôme.	14 Comment s'appelle ton ami?	13 J'ai dix-neuf ans.	12 Mon anniversaire est le cinq novembre.	11 Je suis d'Alger.	10 Je m'appelle Sophie.	9 Elle s'appelle	8 Elle est de
16 D'où est-il?	17 Il est de Toulouse.	18 Quel âge a-t-il?	19 Il a trente ans.	20 Quelle est la date de ton anniversaire?	21 Son anniversaire est le douze mai.	22 Mon amie s'appelle Vanessa.	23 Quel âge a-t-elle?
ARRIVÉE	30 Je suis de Tunis.	29 D'où es-tu?	28 Son anniversaire est le douze novembre.	27 Quelle est la date de son anniversaire?	26 Elle est de Paris.	25 D'où est-elle?	24 Elle a trente-et-un ans.

UNIT 2 – FAST & FURIOUS – ROUND 1

1. Bonjour. _______ tu t' _________?
Hello. What's your name?

2. Salut. ___ _______ Martine et _______ vingt-quatre ans.
Hi. My name is Martine and I am twenty-four years old.

3. Aujourd'hui je suis très _______ et _______.
Today, I am very stressed and annoyed.

4. Je ______ __ Paris.
I am from Paris.

5. Mon amie ____________ Émilie et _____ ____ ___ Rennes.
My friend is called Émilie and she is from Rennes.

	Time 1	Time 2	Time 3	Time 4
Time				
Mistakes				

UNIT 2 – FAST & FURIOUS – ROUND 2

1. Bonjour. _______ s' _________ ton ami?
Hello. What's your friend's name?

2. Salut. _____ ______ s'appelle Jérôme et ____ ____ trente ans.
Hi. My friend is called Jérôme and he is thirty years old.

3. Aujourd'hui il est très _______ mais _______.
Today, he is very tired but happy.

4. Il ______ __ Paris.
He is from Paris.

5. Son _____________ est le treize __________.
His birthday is on the 13th February.

	Time 1	Time 2	Time 3	Time 4
Time				
Mistakes				

ASSESSMENT ROUND

1. Choose the correct translation (you won't need two of the sentences)

a. Comment tu t'appelles?   _____

b. D'où es-tu?   _____

c. Quel âge as-tu?   _____

d. Comment s'appelle ton amie?   _____

e. Quelle est la date de son anniversaire?   _____

1. What is your friend's (m) name?
2. How old are you?
3. Where are you from?
4. What is your friend's (f) name?
5. When is his/her birthday?
6. When is your birthday?
7. What's your name?

2. Fill in the gaps with the missing words

a. Salut! Je m'appelle Christian et ______ trente-et-un ans.

b. Mon _______________ est le vingt-huit avril.

c. Je suis un peu _____________.

d. _________________ Dijon en France.

e. Mon amie ______________ Amandine et elle est de Fécamp.

stressé	s'appelle	anniversaire	je suis de	j'ai

3. Translate the sentences into French

a. My name is Marion and I am 27 years old.

b. My name is Théo and I am from Montpellier.

c. Her birthday is on the 24th September.

d. My friend is called Paula and she is from Tunis.

e. My friend is called Antoine and he is from Rabat.

UNIT 3
Saying where I live and am from

Main grammar focus:

- To use *en / au / à la / aux* + noun

Pop-up grammar:

- Adjectival agreement

UNIT 3

Saying where I live and am from

<table>
<tr><td colspan="6">Où habites-tu? Where do you live?
D'où es-tu? Where are you from?</td></tr>
<tr>
<td rowspan="2">Je m'appelle David et...
My name is David and...</td>
<td rowspan="2">je vis dans
I live in

j'habite dans
I live in</td>
<td>une
a</td>
<td>belle beautiful
grande big
jolie pretty
petite small</td>
<td>maison
house</td>
<td rowspan="2">dans le centre
in the centre

dans la banlieue
on the outskirts

sur la côte
on the coast</td>
</tr>
<tr>
<td>un appartement
a flat</td>
<td colspan="2">dans un bâtiment ancien
in an old building

dans un bâtiment moderne
in a modern building

dans un bâtiment neuf
in a new building</td>
</tr>
<tr>
<td>je suis de
I am from</td>
<td>Biarritz
Brest
Bruxelles
Casablanca
Dakar
Fort-de-France
Libreville
Montréal
Nice
Nouméa
Paris
Saint-Denis
Strasbourg</td>
<td colspan="3">dans le Pays basque southwest region of France
en Bretagne (en France) northwest of France
en Belgique (la capitale) capital of Belgium
au Maroc (sur la côte) coast of Morocco
au Sénégal (la capitale) capital of Senegal
en Martinique (la capitale) capital of Martinique
au Gabon (la capitale) capital of Gabon
au Québec Quebec, Canadian province
en Provence (en France) southeast of France
en Nouvelle Calédonie New Caledonia
en France (la capitale) capital of France
à la Réunion (la capitale) capital of Reunion Island
en Alsace (en France) northeast region of France</td>
</tr>
</table>

MAIN GRAMMAR FOCUS
EN / AU / À LA / AUX

If the country you are referring to is a masculine country, the preposition you will need to use to say *I live IN* is **au**:

J'habite <u>au</u> Maroc.   *I live in Morocco.*
J'habite <u>au</u> Québec.   *I live in Quebec.*

If the country you are referring to is a feminine country or if it starts with a vowel, the preposition you will need to use to say *I live IN* is **en**:

J'habite <u>en</u> France.   *I live in France.*
J'habite <u>en</u> Italie.   *I live in Italy.*

If the country you are referring to is a masculine country that starts with a vowel, the preposition you will need to use to say *I live IN* is **en**:

J'habite <u>en</u> Uruguay.   *I live in Uruguay.*
J'habite <u>en</u> Israël.   *I live in Israel.*

If the country you are referring to is plural, the preposition you will need to use to say *I live IN* is **aux**:

J'habite <u>aux</u> Pays-Bas.   *I live in the Netherlands.*
J'habite <u>aux</u> États-Unis.   *I live in the USA.*

To talk about French departments or masculine regions, you need to use **dans**:

J'habite <u>dans</u> le Pays basque.   *I live in the Basque country.*

To talk about big European islands, you need to use **en** but for smaller islands, you need to use **à**:

J'habite <u>en</u> Corse.   *I live in Corsica.*
J'habite <u>à</u> Ibiza.   *I live in Ibiza.*

If the islands are further away from Europe, the preposition is usually **à**:

J'habite <u>à</u> la Réunion.   *I live in Reunion Island.*

But the exceptions are:

J'habite <u>en</u> Martinique.   *I live in Martinique.*
J'habite <u>en</u> Nouvelle Calédonie.   *I live in New Caledonia.*

1. Match up

en Italie	in the USA
aux États-Unis	in Provence
au Maroc	in Belgium
en Provence	in Italy
à la Réunion	in Quebec
en Belgique	in Morocco
au Québec	in Reunion Island

2. Complete with the missing letters

a. _ n M _ rtin _ q _ e   *in Martinique*

b. a _ G _ b _ n   *in Gabon*

c. _ _ Fr _ nc _   *in France*

d. _ u S _ n _ g _ l   *in Senegal*

e. à _ _ Ré _ ni _ n   *in Reunion Island*

f. a _ x Pa _ s-B _ s   *in the Netherlands*

3. Complete with the missing forms of "au, à la, aux, en, dans"

a. Je suis de Paris ______ France.   *I am from Paris in France.*

b. Je suis de Bruxelles ______ Belgique.   *I am from Brussels in Belgium.*

c. Je suis de Montréal ______ Québec.   *I am from Montreal in Quebec.*

d. Je suis de Biarritz ______ le Pays basque.   *I am from Biarritz in the Basque country.*

e. Je suis de Libreville ______ Gabon.   *I am from Libreville in Gabon.*

f. J'habite ______ États-Unis.   *I live in the USA.*

g. Je suis de Saint-Denis ______ Réunion.   *I am from Saint-Denis in the Reunion Island.*

h. Je suis de Rome ______ Italie.   *I am from Rome in Italy.*

4. Break the flow

a. Bonjour!JesuisdeLilleenFrance.

b. JesuisdeMontréalauQuébec.

c. IlestdeNiceenFrance.

d. ElleestdeStrasbourgenAlsace.

e. MapetitesœurestdeDakarauSénégal.

f. MonamiestdeLibrevilleauGabon.

g. JesuisdeBiarritzdanslePaysbasque.

h. TuesdeNouméaenNouvelleCalédonie.

5. Faulty translation: fix the English

a. J'habite au Maroc.   *You live in Morocco.*

b. Il habite en France.   *He is French.*

c. Elle vit en Alsace.   *She lives in Austria.*

d. Tu vis au Gabon.   *You are from Gabon.*

e. Je vis en Bretagne.   *I am from Brittany.*

f. Il vit aux Pays-Bas?   *Does he live in Prague?*

g. Je vis en Belgique.   *I lived in Belgium.*

h. Il vit au Québec.   *He goes to Quebec.*

6. Choose the correct verb

a. Je **suis** / **est** / **es** de Fécamp en France.

b. Tu **est** / **suis** / **es** de Casablanca au Maroc.

c. Il **es** / **est** / **suis** de Bruxelles en Belgique.

d. Elle **suis** / **es** / **est** de Montréal au Québec.

e. Tu **es** / **suis** / **est** de Rome en Italie.

f. Elle **suis** / **est** / **es** de Brest en Bretagne.

g. Je **es** / **suis** / **est** de Biarritz dans le Pays basque.

h. Il **est** / **es** / **suis** de Libreville au Gabon.

7. Translate into French

a. I am from Brest in Brittany.

b. You are from Nice in France.

c. He is from Brussels in Belgium.

d. She is from Dakar in Senegal.

e. You are from Rome in Italy.

f. I am from Libreville in Gabon.

g. He is from Montreal in Quebec.

h. I am from Strasbourg in Alsace.

8. Complete with the missing adjective.

a. J'habite dans une __________ maison.   *I live in a beautiful house.*

b. J'habite dans un bâtiment __________ .   *I live in an old building.*

c. J'habite dans une __________ maison.   *I live in a big house.*

d. J'habite dans un bâtiment __________ .   *I live in a modern building.*

e. J'habite dans une __________ maison.   *I live in a pretty house.*

f. J'habite dans un bâtiment __________ .   *I live in a new building.*

g. J'habite dans une __________ maison.   *I live in a small house.*

POP-UP GRAMMAR
ADJECTIVES

Adjectives are used to describe a noun. They go after the noun but there are some exceptions: **beau** (*beautiful*), **grand** (*big*), **joli** (*pretty*) and **petit** (*small*).

They must agree with the noun they are describing. They will be written in the masculine form or the feminine form.

If the adjective ends with a consonant in the masculine form, you will need to add an **-e** in the feminine form:

un grand château	*a big castle*	**une grande maison**	*a big house*
un petit bâtiment	*a small building*	**une petite maison**	*a small house*

If the adjective ends with an **-i** in the masculine form, you will need to add an **-e** in the feminine form:

un joli bâtiment	*a pretty building*	**une jolie maison**	*a pretty house*

Beau in the masculine form will become ***belle*** in the feminine form:

un beau bâtiment	*a beautiful building*	**une belle maison**	*a beautiful house*

Ancien (*old*) and **neuf** (*new*) come after the noun and will change in the feminine form:

un bâtiment ancien	*an old building*	**un bâtiment neuf**	*a new building*
une maison ancienne	*an old house*	**une maison neuve**	*a new house*

9. Match up

belle	big
petite	old
moderne	pretty
grande	new
ancien	beautiful
neuf	modern
jolie	small

THE LANGUAGE GYM
GRAMMAR BOOKLET I

10. Slalom translation

Je m'appelle	J'habite	Je m'appelle	Je vis dans	Je m'appelle	J'habite
un bâtiment	Pierre	dans une	Isabelle	dans une	Paul
et je suis de	et je suis de	petite	et je suis de	jolie	moderne
dans la	maison dans	Saint-Denis	Bruxelles	Nice	maison
sur la côte	en Belgique	en Provence	banlieue	à la Réunion	le centre

a. My name is Isabelle and I am from Nice in Provence.

b. I live in a pretty house on the coast.

c. My name is Pierre and I am from Saint-Denis in the Reunion island.

d. I live in a modern building on the outskirts.

e. My name is Paul and I am from Brussels in Belgium.

f. I live in a small house in the centre.

11. Translate into English

a. Je vis dans une jolie maison.

b. J'habite dans un petit appartement.

c. J'habite dans un bâtiment neuf.

d. Je vis dans une maison ancienne.

e. Je vis dans une grande maison.

f. J'habite dans un bâtiment moderne.

g. J'habite dans une petite maison.

h. J'habite dans un bâtiment ancien.

12. Spot and correct the errors

a. J'habite dans un neuf appartement.

b. J'habite dans une joli maison.

c. Je vis dans une grand maison.

d. J'habite dans un bâtiment ancienne.

e. Je vis dans un moderne appartement.

f. J'habite dans une maison petite.

g. J'habite dans un bâtiment modern.

h. J'habite dans une maison grande.

13. Choose the correct answer

a. Je vis dans une **jolie / petite / grande** maison.   *I live in a small house.*

b. J'habite dans un bâtiment **moderne / ancien / neuf**.   *I live in a new building.*

c. J'habite **en France / au Gabon / à la Réunion**.   *I live in Gabon.*

d. J'habite dans une maison **moderne / ancienne / neuve**.   *I live in an old house.*

e. Je vis dans un **joli / petit / grand** bâtiment.   *I live in a pretty building.*

f. J'habite **en Espagne / au Japon / à Bornéo**.   *I live in Spain.*

14. Arrange the words in the correct order.

a. habites Où -tu? — *Where do you live?*

b. Je en France de Toulouse suis — *I am from Toulouse in France.*

c. sur la côte une jolie maison J'habite dans — *I live in a pretty house on the coast.*

d. Je vis dans moderne un appartement — *I live in a modern flat.*

e. dans J'habite une neuve maison centre dans le — *I live in a new house in the centre.*

f. Je suis au Sénégal de Dakar — *I am from Dakar in Senegal.*

g. de Nouméa Je suis en Nouvelle Calédonie — *I am from Nouméa in New Caledonia.*

h. en Alsace de Strasbourg Je suis et une petite je vis dans maison
I am from Starsbourg in Alsace and I live in a small house.

15. Guided translation: complete the translation

a. My name is Paul and I am* 25.   Je ______________ Paul et ______ vingt-cinq ans.

b. I am from Brest in Britany.   Je ________ ___ Brest ___ Bretagne.

c. I am from Nice in Provence.   Je ________ ___ Nice ___ Provence.

d. I live in a big house.   J'__________ dans une ________ maison.

e. I live in a new flat...   Je ______ dans un appartement ___________...

f. ...in a modern building.   ...dans un bâtiment _____________ .

16. Tangled translation

a. **I live in** une petite maison.

b. **I am from** Casablanca au Maroc.

c. Je vis dans **an old building** sur la côte.

d. **Where** habites-tu?

e. D'où **are you from?**

f. J'habite dans une **beautiful house.**

g. Je suis de Fort-de-France **in Martinique.**

h. J'habite dans un **big flat.**

17. Translate into French

a. Where do you live?

b. I live in a small house on the outskirts.

c. Where are you from?

d. I am from Dakar in Senegal.

e. I live in a modern flat.

f. I live in a beautiful house in France.

g. I live in an old building in Quebec.

h. I live in a new building in the Reunion Island.

No Snakes No Ladders

	1	2	3	4	5	6	7
START	My name is David.	I am from Dakar in Senegal.	I live in a big house in the centre.	My friend is called Antoine.	I live in a pretty house on the outskirts.	He is 12.	I live in a flat in an old building.
15 I live in a small house on the outskirts.	**14** How are you?	**13** I am 21.	**12** Today, I am very well.	**11** My brother is called Frédéric.	**10** Where do you live?	**9** My birthday is on the 20th April.	**8** Today, I am tired (m).
16 What is your name?	**17** I live in a beautiful house in the centre.	**18** Thank you.	**19** I live in a flat in a modern building.	**20** What is your brother's name?	**21** Today, I am relaxed (f).	**22** I live in a small house on the coast.	**23** How old are you?
FINISH	**30** How old is she?	**29** Where are you from?	**28** My friend is called Pam.	**27** When is her birthday?	**26** My sister is called Marie.	**25** When is your birthday?	**24** I live in a flat in a new buiding.

No Snakes No Ladders

DÉPART	**1** Je m'appelle David.	**2** Je suis de Dakar au Sénégal.	**3** Je vis dans une grande maison dans le centre.	**4** Mon ami s'appelle Antoine.	**5** J'habite dans une jolie maison dans la banlieue.	**6** Il a douze ans.
7 Je vis dans un appartement dans un bâtiment ancien.	**8** Aujourd'hui je suis fatigué.	**9** Mon anniversaire est le vingt avril.	**10** Où habites-tu?	**11** Mon frère s'appelle Frédéric.	**12** Aujourd'hui ça va très bien.	**13** J'ai vingt-et-un ans.
14 Comment vas-tu?	**15** Je vis dans une petite maison dans la banlieue.	**16** Comment tu t'appelles?	**17** J'habite dans une belle maison dans le centre.	**18** Merci.	**19** J'habite dans un appartement dans un bâtiment moderne.	**20** Comment s'appelle ton frère?
21 Aujourd'hui je suis détendue.	**22** J'habite dans une petite maison sur la côte.	**23** Quel âge as-tu?	**24** Je vis dans un appartement dans un bâtiment neuf.	**25** Quelle est la date de ton anniversaire?	**26** Ma sœur s'appelle Marie.	**27** Quelle est la date de son anniversaire?
28 Mon amie s'appelle Pam.	**29** D'où es-tu?	**30** Quel âge a-t-elle?	**ARRIVÉE**			

UNIT 3 – FAST & FURIOUS – ROUND 1

1. Bonjour. _________ tu t' __________?
    Hello. What's your name?

2. Salut. ___ _________ Claire et _________ vingt-huit ans.
    Hi. My name is Claire and I am twenty-eight years old.

3. Aujourd'hui je suis très _________ mais __________.
    Today, I am very relaxed but sad.

4. Je _______ ___ Paris ____ France
    I am from Paris in France.

5. J'habite dans une ____________ _________ dans le ___________.
    I live in a beautiful house in the centre.

	Time 1	Time 2	Time 3	Time 4
Time				
Mistakes				

UNIT 3 – FAST & FURIOUS – ROUND 2

1. Bonjour. _________ tu t' __________?
    Hello. What's your name?

2. Salut. ___ _________ Alexandre et _________ vingt-deux ans.
    Hi. My name is Alexandre and I am twenty-two years old.

3. Aujourd'hui je suis très _________ mais __________.
    Today, I am very happy but tired.

4. Je _______ ___ Montréal ____ Québec.
    I am from Montreal in Quebec.

5. J'habite dans un ___________ dans un ___________ ___________.
    I live in a flat in an old building.

	Time 1	Time 2	Time 3	Time 4
Time				
Mistakes				

ASSESSMENT ROUND

1. Choose the correct translation (you won't need two of the sentences)

a. J'habite dans une belle maison dans la banlieue. _____

b. Je vis dans un appartement dans un bâtiment neuf. _____

c. Je m'appelle Claire et je suis de Nice en Provence. _____

d. Aujourd'hui, ça va parce que je suis heureuse. _____

e. Où habites-tu? _____

1. Where do you live?
2. Where are you from?
3. I live in a flat in a new building.
4. I live in a pretty house on the outskirts.
5. My name is Claire and I am from Nice in Provence.
6. Today, I am well because I am happy.
7. I live in a beautiful house on the outskirts.

2. Fill in the gaps with the missing words

a. Bonjour! Je m'appelle François. Où ______________-tu?

b. J'habite dans une _________ maison sur la côte. D'où es-tu?

c. Je __________ Bruxelles en Belgique.

d. Je vis dans un appartement dans un bâtiment ___________ dans le centre.

e. Aujourd'hui ça va mal parce que je suis ___________.

suis de	malade	jolie	ancien	habites

3. Translate the sentences into French

a. My name is Marine and I am 30 years old.

b. My name is Damien and I am from Saint-Denis in the Reunion Island.

c. I live in a small house on the coast.

d. I live in a flat in a modern building on the outskirts.

e. Today, I am very bad because I am very stressed.

UNIT 4
Things I like/dislike: school subjects & teachers

Main grammar focus:

- To conjugate ER verbs such as *adorer* / *aimer* in the present indicative

Pop-up grammar:

- To use adjectival agreement

UNIT 4
Things I like/dislike: school subjects & teachers

Quelles matières étudies-tu? *What subjects do you study?*								
Quelle matière tu (n') aimes (pas)? Pourquoi? *Which subject do you (**not**) like? Why?*								
Tu aimes le français? Pourquoi? *Do you like French? Why?*								

Au collège, j'étudie *At school, I study*		**l'allemand / l'histoire / les sciences / etc.**				

J'aime *I like* **Je n'aime pas** *I don't like* **Mon ami(e) aime** *My friend likes* **Mon ami(e) n'aime pas** *My friend does not like*	**l'**	**allemand** *German* **anglais** *English* **espagnol** *Spanish*	**car** *because* **mais** *but*	**c'est** *it is* **ce n'est pas** *it is not*	**amusant** *fun* **compliqué** *complicated* **ennuyeux** *boring* **facile** *easy* **fatigant** *tiring* **intéressant** *interesting* **utile** *useful*
	le	**dessin** *art* **français** *French*			
	l'	**éducation civique** *citizenship* **éducation physique** *PE* **informatique** *ICT* **histoire** *history*			
	la	**chimie** *chemistry* **géographie** *geography*			
	les	**langues** *languages* **mathématiques** *maths* **sciences** *science*			

De plus,	**j'adore ça** *I love it* **j'aime ça** *I like it*	**parce que** *because*	**j'apprends beaucoup** — *I learn a lot* **c'est utile pour le futur** — *it is useful for the future* **j'ai des amis en classe** — *I have friends in class*		
			le professeur est *the teacher (m) is* **la professeure est** *the teacher (f) is*	**assez** *quite* **très** *very*	**amusant(e)** *funny* **bon(ne)** *good* **ennuyeux/euse** *boring* **méchant(e)** *mean* **patient(e)** *patient* **sympathique** *nice*

MAIN GRAMMAR FOCUS
ADORER / AIMER

J'adore	*I love*	J'aime	*I like*
Tu adores	*You love*	**Tu aimes**	*You like*
Il / Elle adore	*He / She loves*	**Il / Elle aime**	*He / She likes*
Nous adorons	*We love*	**Nous aimons**	*We like*
Vous adorez	*You (guys) love*	**Vous aimez**	*You (guys) like*
Ils / Elles adorent	*They love*	**Ils / Elles aiment**	*They like*

1. Match up

j'aime	I don't like
j'adore	you (guys) like
je n'aime pas	my friend likes
nous adorons	I like
mon ami aime	she loves
vous aimez	we love
elle adore	I love

2. Complete with the missing letters

a. J' _ im _ le dessin. *I like art.*

b. J'a _ o _ e la chimie. *I love chemistry.*

c. Tu a _ m _ s l'anglais. *You like English.*

d. Elle _ d _ r _ le français. *She loves French.*

e. Il ai _ _ les langues. *He likes languages.*

f. Tu _ _ _ res les sciences. *You love science.*

3. Complete with the missing verbs

a. J'_________ l'espagnol car c'est facile. *I like Spanish because it is easy.*

b. Nous _________ le dessin car ce n'est pas ennuyeux. *We like art because it is not boring.*

c. J'_________ la chimie mais ce n'est pas utile. *I like chemistry but it isn't useful.*

d. Mon ami _______ le français car c'est amusant. *My friend likes French because it's fun.*

e. Elles _________ les mathématiques. *They love maths.*

f. Tu _________ la géographie? *Do you like geography?*

g. L'informatique? J'_________ ça. *ICT? I love it.*

h. Ils _________ les langues car c'est utile. *They like languages because it is useful.*

4. Break the flow	**5. Faulty translation: fix the English**

4. Break the flow

a. Jaimeléducationphysique.

b. Tuadoreslessciences.

c. Nousnaimonspasl'informatique.

d. Ellesaimentlespagnol.

e. Mapetitesœuradorelefrançais.

f. Vousaimezlachimie.

g. Jenaimepaslallemandetledessin.

h. Tuaimeslhistoire?Jadoreça.

5. Faulty translation: fix the English

a. J'aime l'espagnol.   *I love Spanish.*

b. Il adore la chimie.   *She loves chemistry.*

c. Elle aime le dessin.   *She hates art.*

d. Tu aimes l'anglais.   *He likes English.*

e. Je n'aime pas ça.   *I love it.*

f. Il adore le français.   *He likes French.*

g. Ils aiment l'histoire.   *We like history.*

h. Vous adorez la géo.   *You (guys) like RE.*

6. Choose the correct verb

a. J'**aime / aimes** l'allemand.

b. Tu **aime / aimes** le français?

c. Ils **adores / adorent** l'éducation civique.

d. Elle **n'aime pas / n'aimes pas** la chimie.

e. Tu **adore / adores** l'informatique.

f. Vous **aimez / aimons** l'histoire.

g. La géographie? Nous **adorons / adorez** ça.

h. Il **aime / aimes** l'éducation physique.

7. Translate into French

a. I like science.

b. You love geography.

c. We like French.

d. She loves art.

e. You (guys) like languages.

f. They (f) don't like citizenship.

g. He doesn't like maths.

h. I love English.

8. Complete with the missing adjectives in the masculine or feminine forms

a. J'aime l'éducation physique car c'est ___________.   *I like PE because it is fun.*

b. Je n'aime pas le dessin car c'est ___________.   *I don't like art because it is complicated.*

c. J'aime l'histoire mais ce n'est pas ___________.   *I like history but it isn't easy.*

d. J'aime les langues car c'est ___________.   *I like languages because it is interesting.*

e. Le professeur est très ___________.   *The teacher is very patient.*

f. La professeure est très ___________.   *The teacher is very mean.*

g. La professeure est assez ___________.   *The teacher is quite boring.*

h. Le professeur est assez ___________.   *The teacher is quite good.*

POP-UP GRAMMAR
ADJECTIVES

Adjectives must agree with the noun they are describing.

If the adjective ends with an **-e** in the masculine form, it will stay the same in the feminine form:

Le professeur est sympathique.	*The teacher is nice.*
La professeure est sympathique.	*The teacher is nice.*

If the adjective ends with a consonant in the masculine form, you will need to add an **-e** in the feminine form:

Le professeur est méchant.	*The teacher is mean.*
La professeure est méchant<u>e</u>.	*The teacher is mean.*

The adjective **bon** will double the final consonant in the feminine form:

Le professeur est bon.	*The teacher is good.*
La professeure est bon<u>ne</u>.	*The teacher is good.*

If the adjective ends with **-eux** in the masculine form, it will change to **-euse** in the feminine form:

Le professeur est ennuyeux.	*The teacher is boring.*
La professeure est ennuy<u>euse</u>.	*The teacher is boring.*

When the adjective is introduced by **c'est**, it is always in the masculine form regardless as to the noun it is describing.

J'aime le français car c'est amusant.	*I like French because it is fun.*
J'aime les sciences car c'est amusant.	*I like science because it is fun.*

9. Match up

amusant	complicated
utile	good (f)
fatigant	mean (f)
bonne	fun
méchante	patient (f)
compliqué	useful
patiente	tiring

10. Slalom translation

Au collège,	J'adore	Nous aimons	Mon amie	J'aime ça	J'adore ça
l'informatique	j'étudie	le français	parce que	parce que	n'aime pas
la professeure	mais	l'allemand,	car	les sciences	le prof
car c'est	est	est	l'histoire et	c'est	ce n'est pas
patiente	amusant	difficile	bon	les sciences	utile

a. At school, I study German, history and science.

b. I love French because it is useful.

c. We like ICT but it is not fun.

d. My friend doesn't like science because it is difficult.

e. I like it because the teacher (m) is good.

f. I love it because the teacher (f) is patient.

11. Translate into English

a. J'aime l'allemand car c'est intéressant.

b. Vous adorez le français car c'est amusant.

c. Je n'aime pas la chimie. Ce n'est pas utile.

d. Nous aimons les langues car c'est facile.

e. Le professeur est assez méchant.

f. La professeure est très patiente.

g. Le professeur est très bon.

h. La professeure est assez ennuyeuse.

12. Spot and correct the errors

a. J'étudie la géographie. C'est amusante.

b. Le professeur est ennuyeuse.

c. La professeur est patiente.

d. Le professeur est méchante.

e. Je n'aime pas les sciences. C'est fatigants.

f. La professeure est bon.

g. J'aime l'histoire car c'est intéressante.

h. La professeure est amusant.

13. Choose the correct answer

a. J'aime l'allemand. C'est **amusant / facile / utile**. *I like German. It is useful.*

b. Les langues? C'est **compliqué / facile / intéressant**. *Languages? It's interesting.*

c. Le professeur est **bon / patient / ennuyeux**. *The teacher is good.*

d. Les sciences? C'est **ennuyeux / compliqué / fatigant**. *Science? It's complicated.*

e. La professeure est **patiente / amusante / méchante**. *The teacher is funny.*

f. J'aime l'informatique. C'est **intéressant / utile / facile**. *I like IT. It's easy.*

14. Arrange the words in the correct order.

a. Quelles étudies-tu? matières   *What subjects do you study?*

b. j'étudie Au collège, les langues   *At school, I study languages.*

c. Quelle tu matière aimes?   *Which subject do you like?*

d. J'aime c'est utile car les mathématiques   *I like maths because it is useful.*

e. tu Quelle n'aimes pas matière?   *Which subject do you not like?*

f. Tu la aimes? Pourquoi? géographie   *Do you like geography? Why?*

g. Nous les sciences n'aimons pas car facile ce n'est pas
We don't like science because it is not easy.

h. n'aime pas Mon ami civique l'éducation ce n'est pas car intéressant
My friend does not like citizenship because it is not interesting.

---

15. Guided translation: complete the translation

a. I like art because it is interesting.   J'________ le dessin car c'est ___________ .

b. They don't like PE.   Ils _________ _____ l'éducation physique.

c. My friend (m) likes history.   Mon ______ _________ l'histoire.

d. I love it. The teacher (m) is good.   J'_______ __. Le _____________ est _____ .

e. I like it. The teacher (f) is nice.   J'_______ __. La _____________ est _____ .

f. Do you (guys) like French? Why?   Vous _________ le français? _____________?

---

16. Tangled translation

a. **I study** les langues et les sciences.

b. **They (f) like** le dessin car c'est **fun.**

c. **We don't like** l'histoire car c'est **tiring.**

d. **What** matière tu n'aimes pas?

e. Tu aimes **French? Why?**

f. **I love it** car **it is not** ennuyeux.

g. Le professeur est très **nice.**

h. La professeure est assez **good.**

17. Translate into French

a. What subjects do you study?

b. At school, I study PE and ICT.

c. Which subject do you like?

d. I like Spanish because it is easy.

e. Which subject do you not like?

f. I don't like maths: it isn't fun.

g. The teacher (m) is boring.

h. The teacher (f) is funny.

No Snakes No Ladders

START

1	My name is Antoine.
2	I am from Dakar in Senegal.
3	I live in a big house in the centre.
4	At school, I study art and French.
5	I live in a pretty house on the outskirts.
6	I like science because it is interesting.
7	I live in a flat in an old building.
8	Today, I am tired (m).
9	I don't like PE because it is tiring.
10	Where do you live?
11	My friend (m) likes science but it is complicated.
12	Today, I am very well.
13	I am 21.
14	What subjects do you study?
15	My friend (f) doesn't like chemistry because it's not easy.
16	What is your name?
17	I live in a beautiful house in the centre.
18	Which subject do you like?
19	I live in a flat in a modern building.
20	I like it because the teacher (f) is patient.
21	I love it because the teacher (m) is good.
22	I live in a small house on the coast.
23	How old are you?
24	I live in a flat in a new buiding.
25	Do you like languages? Why?
26	I study history because it is interesting.
27	It is not complicated.
28	I like it because it is not boring.
29	The teacher (f) is funny.
30	The teacher (m) is nice.

FINISH

No Snakes No Ladders

DÉPART	**1** Je m'appelle Antoine.	**2** Je suis de Dakar au Sénégal.	**3** J'habite dans une grande maison dans le centre.	**4** Au collège, j'étudie le dessin et le français.	**5** J'habite dans une jolie maison dans la banlieue.	**6** J'aime les sciences car c'est intéressant.	**7** J'habite dans un appartement dans un bâtiment ancien.
15 Mon amie n'aime pas la chimie car ce n'est pas facile.	**14** Quelles matières étudies-tu?	**13** J'ai vingt-et-un ans.	**12** Aujourd'hui ça va très bien.	**11** Mon ami aime les sciences mais c'est compliqué.	**10** Où habites-tu?	**9** Je n'aime pas l'éducation physique car c'est fatigant.	**8** Aujourd'hui je suis fatigué.
16 Comment t'appelles-tu?	**17** J'habite dans une belle maison dans le centre.	**18** Quelle matière tu aimes?	**19** J'habite dans un appartement dans un bâtiment moderne.	**20** J'aime ça parce que la professeure est patiente.	**21** J'adore ça parce que le professeur est bon.	**22** J'habite dans une petite maison sur la côte.	**23** Quel âge as-tu?
ARRIVÉE	**30** Le professeur est sympathique.	**29** La professeure est amusante.	**28** J'aime ça car ce n'est pas ennuyeux.	**27** Ce n'est pas compliqué.	**26** J'étudie l'histoire car c'est intéressant.	**25** Tu aimes les langues? Pourquoi?	**24** J'habite dans un appartement dans un bâtiment neuf.

UNIT 4 – FAST & FURIOUS – ROUND 1

1.   Bonjour. __________ matières ____________-tu?
   Hello. What subjects do you study?

2.   Salut. Au collège, j'____________ le ____________ et l'____________.
   Hi. At school, I study French and Spanish.

3.   J'____________ le ____________ car c'____________ facile et ce n'est pas ____________.
   I like French because it is easy and it is not boring.

4.   L'espagnol? Elles ____________ ça parce que le ____________ est ____________.
   Spanish? They love it because the teacher is funny.

5.   J'habite dans une ____________ ____________ dans le ____________.
   I live in a small house in the centre.

	Time 1	Time 2	Time 3	Time 4
Time				
Mistakes				

UNIT 4 – FAST & FURIOUS – ROUND 2

1.   Bonjour. __________ matières ____________-tu?
   Hello. What subjects do you study?

2.   Salut. Au collège, j'____________ le ____________ et les ____________.
   Hi. At school, I study art and languages.

3.   J'____________ les ____________ car c'____________ intéressant et ce n'est pas ____________.
   I like languages because it is interesting and it is not complicated.

4.   Le dessin? Ils ____________ ça parce que la ____________ est ____________.
   Art? They like it because the teacher is patient.

5.   J'habite dans une ____________ ____________ sur la ____________.
   I live in a pretty house on the coast.

	Time 1	Time 2	Time 3	Time 4
Time				
Mistakes				

ASSESSMENT ROUND

1. Choose the correct translation (you won't need two of the sentences)

a. Au collège, j'étudie les langues et l'éducation civique   .   _____

b. Quelle matière tu aimes?   _____

c. J'aime la géographie car c'est utile.   _____

d. Mon ami n'aime pas l'histoire car ce n'est pas amusant.   _____

e. Le professeur est assez sympathique.   _____

1. My friend doesn't like history because it is not fun.
2. Which subject do you like?
3. The teacher is very nice.
4. At school, I study languages and citizenship.
5. The teacher is quite nice.
6. Which subjects do you study?
7. I like geography because it is useful.

2. Fill in the gaps with the missing words

a. Au collège, j'___________ les mathématiques et l'éducation physique.

b. Quelles matières ___________-tu?

c. J'aime la chimie car c'est facile et ___________ compliqué.

d. Mon amie n'aime pas les __________ car ce n'est pas facile.

e. La professeure est assez ___________ .

ce n'est pas	étudies	ennuyeuse	étudie	langues

3. Translate the sentences into French

a. My name is Patricia and I am 23 years old.

b. My name is Claude and I am from Nouméa in New Caledonia.

c. I live in a beautiful house on the coast.

d. We like German because it is useful but we don't like science because it is not easy.

e. I love it because the teacher (f) is very good.

UNIT 5
Things I like/dislike: free time

Main grammar focus:

- To use *aimer / adorer / détester* in the present indicative + infinitive

Pop-up grammar:

- To use *c'est* followed by an adjective

THE LANGUAGE GYM
GRAMMAR BOOKLET I

UNIT 5
Things I like/dislike: free time

Qu'est-ce que tu aimes faire pendant ton temps libre?			*What do you like to do in your free time?*

			à la pêche — *fishing*	

		aller *to go*	**à la pêche** *fishing*	
Pendant mon temps libre *In my free time*	**j'adore** *I love*		**à la piscine** *to the pool* **au centre commercial** *to the shopping mall* **au centre sportif** *to the sports centre* **au gymnase** *to the gym* **au parc** *to the park* **chez mon ami(e)** *to my friend's house* **me promener** *for a walk*	**avec ma sœur** *with my sister* **avec mes amis** *with my friends*
	j'aime *I like*	**faire** *to do*	**de la natation** *swimming* **de la randonnée** *hiking* **de l'équitation** *horse riding* **du footing** *jogging* **du sport** *sport* **du vélo** *cycling*	**avec mes parents** *with my parents* **avec mon ami Pierre** *with my friend Pierre* **avec mon frère** *with my brother*
Quand j'ai du temps libre *When I have free time*	**je déteste** *I hate*	**jouer** *to play*	**à la PlayStation** **au basket** *basketball* **au foot** *football* **au tennis** *tennis* **aux cartes** *cards* **aux échecs** *chess* **aux jeux vidéo** *videogames* **sur l'ordinateur** *on the computer*	

J'aime cela *I like it* **Je n'aime pas cela** *I don't like it*	**car/parce que** *because*	**c'est** *it is* **ce n'est pas** *it is not*	**amusant** *fun* **ennuyeux** *boring* **fatigant** *tiring* **génial** *great* **intéressant** *interesting* **sain** *healthy*

MAIN GRAMMAR FOCUS
ADORER / AIMER / DÉTESTER + INFINITIVE

J'adore	J'aime	Je déteste
I love	*I like*	*I hate*
Tu adores	**Tu aimes**	**Tu détestes**
You love	*You like*	*You hate*
Il/Elle adore	**Il/Elle aime**	**Il/Elle déteste**
He/She loves	*He/She likes*	*He/She hates*
Nous adorons	**Nous aimons**	**Nous détestons**
We love	*We like*	*We hate*
Vous adorez	**Vous aimez**	**Vous détestez**
You (guys) love	*You (guys) like*	*You (guys) hate*
Ils/Elles adorent	**Ils/Elles aiment**	**Ils/Elles détestent**
They love	*They like*	*They hate*

When **adorer, aimer** and **détester** are followed by a verb, it must be in the infinitive form.

J'adore <u>aller</u> au parc.	*I love <u>to go</u> to the park.*
J'aime <u>jouer</u> au tennis.	*I like <u>to play</u> tennis.*
Je déteste <u>faire</u> du vélo.	*I hate <u>to do</u> cycling.*

1. Match up

nous aimons jouer	I hate to do
ils adorent aller	I don't like it
je déteste faire	she likes it
tu n'aimes pas	they love to go
je n'aime pas cela	I love to play
j'adore jouer	you don't like
elle aime cela	we like to play

2. Complete with the missing letters

a. J' _ im _ _ ll _ r au p _ rc.
I like to go to the park.

b. J'a _ o _ e j _ _ er au t _ nn _ s.
I love to play tennis.

c. J'a _ m _ f _ _ r _ d _ vél _.
I like to do cycling.

d. Il dét _ st _ _ ll _ r s _ pr _ m _ n _ r.
He hates to go for a walk.

3. Complete with the missing infinitive *aller, faire, jouer*

a. J'aime ____________ me promener.　　　　*I like to go for a walk.*

b. Elle déteste ____________ au foot.　　　　*She hates to play football.*

c. J'aime ____________ de l'équitation.　　　　*I like to do horse riding.*

d. Nous adorons ____________ à la piscine.　　　　*We like to go to the pool.*

e. Vous détestez ____________ au gymnase.　　　　*You (guys) hate to go to the gym.*

f. J'adore ____________ de la randonnée.　　　　*I like to do hiking.*

g. Tu n'aimes pas ____________ aux échecs.　　　　*You don't like to play chess.*

h. Ils aiment ____________ du vélo.　　　　*They like to do cycling.*

4. Break the flow

a. Jaimefairedufooting.

b. Jadorejouerauxéchecs.

c. Ilsdétestentalleraugymnase.

d. Tuaimesfairedelanatation.

e. Mapetitesœuradoreralleràlapiscine.

f. Nousaimonsjouerauxjeuxvidéo.

g. Jenaimepasallerauparc.

h. Vousaimezfairedusport?

5. Faulty translation: fix the English

a. J'aime aller au parc.
I love to go to the park.

b. Elles adorent faire du vélo.
She loves to do cycling.

c. Elle aime faire de l'équitation.
She hates to do horse riding.

d. Tu aimes jouer aux cartes.
You like to play chess.

e. Vous détestez aller au centre commercial.
You (guys) love to go to the shopping mall.

6. Choose the correct verb

a. J'**aime / aimes** jouer au foot.

b. Tu **aime / aimes** aller au centre sportif?

c. Il **adores / adore** faire du sport.

d. Elle **n'aime pas / n'aimes pas** jouer au basket.

e. Nous **adorez / adorons** faire de la natation.

f. Elles **aimes / aiment** aller à la pêche.

g. Le footing? Vous **aimez / aimes** cela.

h. Ils **détestent / détestes** aller se promener.

7. Translate into French

a. I like to go fishing.

b. You (guys) love to do swimming.

c. He likes to play basketball.

d. They (m) love to go for a walk.

e. You like to do cycling.

f. We hate to play on the computer.

g. He likes to go to the gym.

h. You (guys) hate to do hiking.

8. Complete with the missing adjective

a. Nous aimons aller au centre sportif car c'est _______________ .
We like to go to the sports centre because it is fun.

b. Je déteste jouer aux échecs parce que c'est _______________ .
I hate to play chess because it is boring.

c. Tu aimes faire de la randonnée car c'est _______________ .
You like to go hiking because it is healthy.

d. Elles adorent faire de la natation parce que c'est _______________ .
They like to do swimming because it is great.

e. Je déteste aller me promener car ce n'est pas _______________ .
I hate to go for a walk because it is not interesting.

f. J'adore aller chez mon ami car c'est _______________ .
I like to go to my friend's house because it is great.

g. Vous n'aimez pas jouer aux jeux vidéo parce que ce n'est pas _______________ .
You (guys) don't like to play video games because it is not healthy.

h. J'aime faire du sport parce que ce n'est pas _______________ .
I like to do sport because it is not boring.

POP-UP GRAMMAR
C'EST + ADJECTIVES

Adjectives are used to describe a noun.

When the adjective is introduced by **c'est**, it is always in the masculine form regardless as to the noun it is describing.

J'aime aller à la pêche car c'est amusant.
I like to go fishing because it is fun.

J'adore faire de la natation car c'est sain.
I love to do swimming because it is healthy.

Je déteste jouer aux cartes car c'est ennuyeux.
I hate to play cards because it is boring.

9. Match up

amusant	interesting
c'est	it is not
fatigant	boring
ce n'est pas	fun
sain	it is
intéressant	healthy
ennuyeux	tiring

10. Slalom translation

Qu'est-ce que	J'aime aller	J'adore jouer	Ils détestent	J'aime cela	Je déteste ça
jouer au	tu aimes	car c'est	car	à la piscine	aux échecs
parce que	assez	car	faire pendant	basket car	ce n'est pas
amusant et	c'est	ce n'est pas	génial et	c'est	ton
intéressant	intéressant	temps libre?	génial	sain	amusant

a. What do you like to do in your free time?

b. I like to go to the pool because it is fun.

c. I love to play chess because it is interesting.

d. They hate to play basketball because it isn't great.

e. I like it because it is quite fun and healthy.

f. I hate it because it isn't great and interesting.

11. Translate into English

a. Qu'est-ce que tu aimes faire?

b. Elles aiment aller à la pêche.

c. Vous détestez faire du sport.

d. Elle adore jouer aux cartes.

e. Nous aimons cela car c'est amusant.

f. Ils n'aiment pas cela car ce n'est pas sain.

g. Tu aimes cela car ce n'est pas fatigant.

h. J'adore faire du footing car c'est génial.

12. Spot and correct the errors

a. J'aime faire au basket.

b. Ils détestent jouer de la randonnée.

c. Qu'est-ce que tu faire aimes?

d. J'adore aller de la natation.

e. Vous aimez cela car cest amusant.

f. Je ne aime pas cela car c'est ennuyeux.

g. J'aime aller à la pêche car c'est géniale.

h. Vous adorez chez votre ami aller.

13. Choose the correct answer

a. J'aime aller **à la pêche / au parc / me promener**.   *I like to go to the park.*

b. Elle adore jouer **aux cartes / au foot / au tennis**.   *She loves to play cards.*

c. Il déteste faire du **footing / sport / vélo**.   *He hates to do cycling.*

d. J'aime cela. C'est **sain / amusant / génial**.   *I like it. It's fun.*

e. Je n'aime pas cela. C'est **ennuyeux / fatigant / barbant**.   *I don't like it. It's tiring.*

f. J'aime aller **à la piscine / au gymnase / au parc**.   *I like to go to the gym.*

14. Arrange the words in the correct order

a. du temps libre quand j'ai   *When I have free time*

b. aller au parc j'adore   *I love to go to the park*

c. mon temps pendant libre   *In my free time*

d. de l'équitation ils aiment faire   *They like to do horse riding*

e. au centre commercial nous détestons aller   *We hate to go to the shopping mall*

f. au centre sportif vous aimez aller   *You (guys) like to go to the sports centre*

g. cela ce n'est pas parce que fatigant j'aime   *I like it because it is not tiring*

h. cela sain parce que je n'aime pas ce n'est pas   *I don't like it because it is not healthy*

i. parce que tu aimes cela amusant c'est   *You like it because it is fun*

15. Tangled translation

a. Qu'est-ce que **you like** faire?

b. **I like to play** au foot parce que c'est **fun.**

c. **I don't like** aller au parc car c'est **tiring.**

d. **We love to do** du vélo car c'est **healthy.**

e. Tu aimes **play chess? Why?**

f. **I like it** car **it is not** ennuyeux.

g. **You (guys) don't like it** car **it is** sain.

h. Il aime **to do swimming** car c'est **great.**

16. Translate into French

a. You (guys) hate to do horse riding…

b. …because it is not fun.

c. I love to go to my friend's house…

d. …because it is great.

e. He likes to play on the PlayStation…

f. …because it isn't boring.

g. They (f) like it because it is interesting.

h. I don't like it because it is not healthy.

UNIT 5 – ORAL PING PONG – Person A

ENGLISH	FRENCH	ENGLISH	FRENCH
I love to go fishing.	J'adore aller à la pêche.	I hate to do jogging.	Je déteste faire du footing.
We like to do swimming.		I like to go to the gym.	
I hate to play basketball.	Je déteste jouer au basket.	I love to play chess.	J'adore jouer aux échecs.
I like it because it is fun.		In my free time, I like to go for a walk with my friends.	
I don't like it because it is not interesting.	Je n'aime pas cela car ce n'est pas intéressant.	You (guys) like it because it is healthy.	Vous aimez cela parce que c'est sain.
What do you like to do in your free time?		When I have free time, I hate to play cards with my sister.	
In my free time, I love to do hiking.	Pendant mon temps libre, j'adore faire de la randonnée.	I don't like it because it is not fun.	Je n'aime pas cela car ce n'est pas amusant.
When I have free time, I like to go to my friend's house.		I like to go to the shopping mall with my friends.	
I love to go to the park with my brother.	J'adore aller au parc avec mon frère.	What do you like to do in your free time?	Qu'est-ce que tu aimes faire pendant ton temps libre?
I like to do cycling with my parents.		I hate to play on the computer.	

UNIT 5 – ORAL PING PONG – Person B

ENGLISH	FRENCH	ENGLISH	FRENCH
I love to go fishing.		I hate to do jogging.	
We like to do swimming.	Nous aimons faire de la natation.	I like to go to the gym.	J'aime aller au gymnase.
I hate to play basketball.		I love to play chess.	
I like it because it is fun.	J'aime cela parce que c'est amusant.	In my free time, I like to go for a walk with my friends.	Pendant mon temps libre, j'aime aller me promener avec mes amis.
I don't like it because it is not interesting.		You (guys) like it because it is healthy.	
What do you like to do in your free time?	Qu'est-ce que tu aimes faire pendant ton temps libre?	When I have free time, I hate to play cards with my sister.	Quand j'ai du temps libre, je déteste jouer aux cartes avec ma sœur.
In my free time, I love to do hiking.		I don't like it because it is not fun.	
When I have free time, I like to go to my friend's house.	Quand j'ai du temps libre, j'aime aller chez mon ami.	I like to go to the shopping mall with my friends.	J'aime aller au centre commercial avec mes amis.
I love to go to the park with my brother.		What do you like to do in your free time?	
I like to do cycling with my parents.	J'aime faire du vélo avec mes parents.	I hate to play on the computer.	Je déteste jouer sur l'ordinateur.

No Snakes No Ladders

START	**1** I love to go fishing.	**2** She likes to do swimming.	**3** I hate to play on the PlayStation.	**4** I love to do hiking.	**5** They like to play basketball.	**6** I hate to go to the pool.	**7** I love to play football.
15 I like to play chess.	**14** We don't like it because it isn't fun.	**13** I like to go for a walk.	**12** I don't like it because it is boring.	**11** I love to do horse riding.	**10** I like it because it is fun.	**9** He hates to do hiking.	**8** I like to go to the shopping mall.
16 I don't like it because it is tiring.	**17** I hate to play tennis.	**18** What do you like to do?	**19** I like it because it is great.	**20** We like to play on the computer.	**21** I hate to go to the sports centre.	**22** I like it because it isn't boring.	**23** I like to go the gym.
FINISH	**30** I like to play cards.	**29** I like it because it is healthy.	**28** You (guys) hate to do sport.	**27** I like to go to the park.	**26** I like it because it isn't tiring.	**25** I love to do cycling.	**24** I don't like it because it isn't interesting.

No Snakes No Ladders

7 – J'adore jouer au foot.	6 – Je déteste aller à la piscine.	5 – Ils aiment jouer au basket.	4 – J'adore faire de la randonnée.	3 – Je déteste jouer à la PlayStation.	2 – Elle aime faire de la natation.	1 – J'adore aller à la pêche.
8 – J'aime aller au centre commercial.	9 – Il déteste faire de la randonnée.	10 – J'aime cela parce que c'est amusant.	11 – J'adore faire de l'équitation.	12 – Je n'aime pas cela car c'est ennuyeux.	13 – J'aime aller me promener.	14 – Nous n'aimons pas cela car ce n'est pas amusant.
23 – J'aime aller au gymnase.	22 – J'aime cela car ce n'est pas ennuyeux.	21 – Je déteste aller au centre sportif.	20 – Nous aimons jouer sur l'ordinateur.	19 – J'aime cela car c'est génial.	18 – Qu'est-ce que tu aimes faire?	17 – Je déteste jouer au tennis.
24 – Je n'aime pas cela car ce n'est pas intéressant.	25 – J'adore faire du vélo.	26 – J'aime cela car ce n'est pas fatigant.	27 – J'aime aller au parc.	28 – Vous détestez faire du sport.	29 – J'aime cela car c'est sain.	30 – J'aime jouer aux cartes.
	15 – J'aime jouer aux échecs. **DÉPART**					16 – Je n'aime pas cela car c'est fatigant.
						ARRIVÉE

UNIT 5 – FAST & FURIOUS – ROUND 1

1.   Bonjour. Qu'est-ce que tu _________ faire pendant ton temps libre?
Hello. What do you like to do in your free time?

2.   Pendant mon temps libre, j'_________ _________ chez mon ami.
During my free time, I love to go to my friend's house.

3.   J'_________ cela parce que c'est _________.
I like it because it is fun.

4.   Quand j'ai du temps libre, je _________ faire de l'_________.
When I have free time, I hate to do horse riding.

5.   Je _________ _____ cela car _____ _____ _____ intéressant.
I don't like it because it isn't interesting.

	Time 1	Time 2	Time 3	Time 4
Time				
Mistakes				

UNIT 5 – FAST & FURIOUS – ROUND 2

1.   Bonjour. Qu'est-ce que tu aimes _________ pendant ton temps libre?
Hello. What do you like to do in your free time?

2.   Pendant mon temps libre, j'adore _________ aux jeux vidéo.
During my free time, I love to play videogames.

3.   J'_________ cela parce que c'est _________.
I like it because it is fun.

4.   Quand j'ai du temps libre, je _________ aller à la _________.
When I have free time, I hate to go fishing.

5.   Je _________ _____cela car _____ _____ _____ amusant.
I don't like it because it isn't fun.

	Time 1	Time 2	Time 3	Time 4
Time				
Mistakes				

ASSESSMENT ROUND

1. Choose the correct translation (you won't need two of the sentences)

a. Qu'est-ce que tu aimes faire pendant ton temps libre?   _____

b. J'aime faire de la randonnée avec mes parents.   _____

c. Je déteste jouer aux échecs avec mon frère.   _____

d. J'aime cela parce que c'est très intéressant.   _____

e. Je n'aime pas cela car ce n'est pas amusant.   _____

1.   I hate to play chess with my brother.
2.   I like this because it is quite interesting.
3.   What do you do in your free time?
4.   I don't like it because it is not fun.
5.   I like to do hiking with my parents.
6.   What do you like to do in your free time?
7.   I like it because it is very interesting.

2. Fill in the gaps with the missing words

a. Pendant mon temps libre, j'_____________ me promener.

b. J'aime cela parce que _____________ assez génial.

c. Quand j'ai du temps libre, je déteste _____________ au gymnase.

d. Je n'aime pas cela car _____________ amusant.

e. Je déteste jouer aux _____________ .

c'est	cartes	aller	adore	ce n'est pas

3. Translate the sentences into French

a. What do you like to do in your free time?

b. In my free time, I love to do cycling.

c. I like it because it is healthy and it is not boring.

d. When I have free time, I hate to go fishing.

e. I don't like it because it is tiring and it is not interesting.

"

UNIT 6
Talking about my family members, saying their age and how well I get on with them.

Main grammar focus:

- Review of *être* + using possessive adjectives (mon, ton, son)

Pop-up grammar:

- To conjugate *s'entendre*

UNIT 6
Talking about my family members, saying their age and how well I get on with them.

Combien de personnes il y a dans ta famille?	How many people are there in your family?
Avec qui tu t'entends bien dans ta famille?	Who do you get on well with in your family?
Tu t'entends mal avec quelqu'un?	Do you get on badly with anyone?

			un *1*	an
Dans ma famille, j'ai *In my family, I have…*	**mon cousin, Tanguy.** *my cousin, Tanguy.*	**Il a**	deux	
	mon grand-père, Léon. *my grandfather Léon.*		trois	
	mon père, Jean. *my father Jean.*		quatre	
	mon oncle, Yvan. *my uncle Yvan.*		cinq six sept huit	
Il y a <u>quatre</u> personnes dans ma famille *There are <u>four</u> people in my family…*	**mon frère aîné, Ronan.** *my older brother Ronan.*		neuf dix onze *11*	
	mon frère cadet, Olivier. *my younger brother Olivier.*		douze *12* treize *13* quatorze *14* quinze *15*	
			seize *16* dix-sept *17*	
Je m'entends bien avec… *I get on well with…*	**ma cousine, Claire.** *my (girl) cousin Claire.*		dix-huit *18* dix-neuf *19* vingt *20*	
	ma grand-mère, Adeline. *my grandmother Adeline.*		vingt-et-un *21* vingt-deux *22* trente *30*	
	ma mère, Anne. *my mother Anne.*	**Elle a**	trente-et-un *31* trente-deux *32* quarante *40*	ans
Je ne m'entends pas bien avec… *I don't get on well with…*	**ma tante, Gisèle.** *my aunt Gisèle.*		cinquante *50* soixante *60* soixante-dix *70*	
	ma sœur aînée, Léa. *my older sister Léa.*		quatre-vingts *80* quatre-vingt-dix *90* cent *100*	
	ma sœur cadette, Sophie. *my younger sister Sophie.*			

MAIN GRAMMAR FOCUS
POSSESSIVE ADJECTIVES

We use possessive adjectives (*my, your, his, her*) to show that something belongs to someone or for relations and friends.

Mon frère   *My* brother

They agree with the noun that follows them.

	Masculine singular	Feminine singular	Plural
My	mon	ma	mes
Your	ton	ta	tes
His / Her	son	sa	ses
Our	notre	notre	nos
Your	votre	votre	vos
Their	leur	leur	leurs

Je m'entends bien avec <u>mon</u> père.
I get on well with <u>my</u> father.

Tu t'entends bien avec <u>ta</u> mère.
You get on well with <u>your</u> mother.

Il s'entend bien avec <u>ses</u> parents.
He gets on well with <u>his</u> parents.

Ils s'entendent bien avec leur chat.
They get on well with their cat.

When *my, your, his/her* is followed by a feminine noun that starts with a vowel, we use **mon, ton, son** in the feminine singular form.

Je m'entends bien avec <u>mon</u> amie.
I get on well with <u>my</u> friend. (f)

Je m'entends bien avec <u>ton</u> amie.
I get on well with <u>your</u> friend. (f)

<table>
<tr><td>

1. Match up

ta tante	my uncle
vos parents	their mother
mon oncle	your aunt
ton frère	his/her friends
nos amies	your brother
ses amis	your parents
leur mère	our friends (f)

</td><td>

2. Complete with the missing letters

a. Je m'entends bien avec l _ _ r c _ _ s _ n.
I get on well with their cousin.

b. Je ne m'entends pas bien avec t _ s _ _ r.
I don't get on with your sister.

c. Dans ma famille j'ai m _ n fr _ r _ c _ d _ t.
In my family, I have my younger brother.

d. Je m'entends bien avec t _ m _ r _.
I get on well with your mother.

</td></tr>
</table>

3. Complete with the correct form of my, your, his/her, our, your, their

a. Je m'entends bien avec ___________ cousin. *I get on well with my cousin.*

b. Je ne m'entends pas bien avec ___________ sœur. *I don't get on well with their sister.*

c. Je m'entends bien avec ___________ cousins. *I get on well with your cousins.*

d. Je ne m'entends pas bien avec ___________ copain. (m) *I don't get on well with his friend.*

e. Je m'entends bien avec ___________ chiens. *I get on well with our dogs.*

f. Je ne m'entends pas bien avec ___________ cheval. (m) *I don't get on well with his horse.*

g. Je m'entends bien avec ___________ tante. *I get on well with your aunt.*

h. Je ne m'entends pas bien avec ___________ oncles. *I don't get on well with her uncles.*

<table>
<tr><td>

4. Break the flow

a. Dansmafamillejaimonpèreetmamère.

b. Jementendsbienavecmonfrèreaîné.

c. Jenementendspasbienavectonpère.

d. Dansmafamillejaimononcleetmatante.

e. Jementendsbienavecleurgrand-père.

f. Jenementendspasbienavecvotrecousine.

g. Dansmafamillejaimonfrèreetmasœur.

h. Jementendsbienavectasœurcadette.

</td><td>

5. Faulty translation: fix the English

a. Je m'entends bien avec ma cousine.
I get on well with your cousin.

b. Dans ma famille j'ai mon grand-père.
In my family, I have my grandmother.

c. Je ne m'entends pas bien avec leur frère.
I don't get on well with his brother.

d. Dans ma famille j'ai mon frère cadet.
In my family, I have my older brother.

e. Je m'entends bien avec son oncle.
I get on well with your uncle.

</td></tr>
</table>

6. Choose the correct possessive adjective	**7. Translate into French**
a. Je m'entends bien avec **ma / mon** mère.	a. In my family, I have my aunt.
b. Dans ma famille, j'ai **ma / mon** frère.	b. I get on well with his cousin. (f)
c. Je m'entends bien avec **ton / ta** mère.	c. In my family, I have my brother.
d. Je ne m'entends pas bien avec **son / sa** sœur.	d. I get on well with your sister.
e. Dans ma famille, j'ai **mon / ma** grand-père.	e. In my family, I have my mother.
f. Je ne m'entends pas bien avec **votre / vos** amie.	f. I get on well with their father.
g. Je m'entends bien avec **mon / mes** frères.	g. In my family, I have my uncle.
h. Je m'entends bien avec **leurs / leur** parents.	h. I get on well with your aunt.

POP-UP GRAMMAR
S'ENTENDRE

We use **s'entendre** to say how we get on with someone. It is a reflexive verb.

Here is how it is conjugated in the present tense:

Je (ne) m'entends (pas)	*I (don't) get on*
Tu (ne) t'entends (pas)	*You (don't) get on*
Il/Elle (ne) s'entend (pas)	*He/She gets on (He/She doesn't get on)*
Nous (ne) nous entendons (pas)	*We (don't) get on*
Vous (ne) vous entendez (pas)	*You (guys) get on (You (guys) don't get on)*
Ils/Elles (ne) s'entendent (pas)	*They (don't) get on*

8. Match up

Je m'entends bien avec ma mère.	We get on well with his aunt.
Tu t'entends bien avec ton frère.	They don't get on well with their sister.
Nous nous entendons bien avec sa tante.	You guys don't get on well with your father.
Elle s'entend bien avec sa grand-mère.	I get on well with my mother.
Ils ne s'entendent pas bien avec leur sœur.	You don't get on well with your uncle.
Tu ne t'entends pas bien avec ton oncle.	You get on well with your brother.
Vous ne vous entendez pas bien avec votre père.	She gets on well with her grandmother.

9. Complete with the correct form of s'entendre

a. Je _______________ bien avec ton frère.   *I get on well with your brother.*

b. Tu _______________ bien avec ta mère.   *You get on well with your mother.*

c. Nous _______________ bien avec nos cousins.   *We get on well with our cousins.*

d. Il ne _______________ pas bien avec ma sœur.   *He doesn't get on well with my sister.*

e. Vous _______________ bien avec vos frères.   *You (guys) get on well with your brothers.*

f. Je ne _______________ pas bien avec mon oncle.   *I don't get on well with my uncle.*

g. Elles _______________ bien avec leur tante.   *They get on well with their aunt.*

h. Elle ne _______________ pas bien avec ses tantes.   *She doesn't get on well with her aunts.*

---

10. Slalom translation

Tu	Chez moi	Je m'entends	Il s'entend	Elle s'entend	Je m'entends
bien avec	bien avec	t'entends	bien avec	j'ai	bien avec
mon chien,	mon père	ses copains	ses frères	bien avec	ton oncle
et	et	et	ton	et	mon chat et
ses sœurs	ma mère	ses profs	mes parents	ta tante	oncle?

a. Do you get on well with your uncle?

b. At home, I have my dog, my cat and my parents.

c. I get on well with my father and my mother.

d. He gets on well with his brothers and his sisters.

e. She gets on well with her friends and her teachers.

f. I get on get with your uncle and your aunt.

<table>
<tr><td>

11. Translate into English

a. Tu t'entends bien avec ta sœur?

b. Je m'entends bien avec mon chat.

c. Il s'entend bien avec son copain.

d. Nous nous entendons bien avec sa copine.

e. Je ne m'entends pas bien avec ton père.

f. Ils s'entendent bien avec leurs pingouins.

g. Elles ne s'entendent pas bien avec vos amis.

h. Vous vous entendez bien avec vos parents.

</td><td>

12. Spot and correct the errors

a. Je m'entends bien avec mon copains.

b. Vous vous entendons bien avec vos frères.

c. Dans ma famille, j'ai mon sœur.

d. Tu t'entends bien avec ta père.

e. Ils ne s'entends pas bien avec leurs profs.

f. Je ne m'entends pas bien avec ma oncle.

g. Nous entendons bien avec notre cousin.

h. Elle ne se entend pas bien avec moi.

</td></tr>
</table>

13. Choose the correct answer

a. J'ai mes **parents / frères / cousins**.　　　　*I have my brothers.*

b. J'ai **mon frère / ma sœur / ma cousine**.　　　*I have my sister.*

c. J'ai **mon père / ma mère / mes sœurs**.　　　*I have my father.*

d. Je m'entends bien avec **ma sœur / mes frères / ta sœur**.　*I get on well with your sister.*

e. Il s'entend bien avec sa **sœur / tante / mère**.　　*He gets on well with his aunt.*

f. Nous nous entendons bien avec ta **sœur / mère / tante**.　*We get on well with your mother.*

14. Arrange the words in the correct order.

a. Tu bien t'entends tes avec parents?　　*Do you get on well with your parents?*

b. Tu mal avec t'entends quelqu'un?　　*Do you get on badly with anyone?*

c. Je avec ne m'entends pas mon père bien.　　*I don't get on well with my father.*

d. Ils avec sœurs s'entendent mes bien.　　*They get on well with my sisters.*

e. Il pas sa ne s'entend grand-mère bien avec.　　*He does not get on well with his grandmother.*

f. Dans sa famille, son père elle a et ses chiens.　　*In her family, she has her father and her dogs.*

g. J'ai, et mon père ma mère mes sœurs.　　*I have my father, my mother and my sisters.*

h. Vous pas bien ne vous entendez avec mère ma.　　*You (guys) don't get on well with my mother.*

15. Tangled translation

a. **You get on well** avec ta sœur.

b. Tu t'entends bien **with your parents?**

c. **I get on well** avec **your uncle.**

d. Dans ma famille, **I have** mes parents.

e. **You (guys) get on well** avec votre tante.

f. **He gets on well** avec **his** grands-parents.

g. **I don't get on** bien avec **your brothers.**

h. Ils **don't get on well** avec **their sister.**

16. Translate into French

a. Do you get on well with your aunt?

b. At home, I have my parents.

c. They (f) get on well with their father.

d. He gets on well with his aunts.

e. You (guys) get on well with my mother.

f. We don't get on well with his friends.

g. I don't get on well with your brother.

h. I get on well with your older sister.

No Snakes No Ladders

START	1	2	3	4	5	6	7
	I get on well with my brother.	I don't get on with your father.	You get on well with your older brother.	You don't get on well with your sister.	Her mother is called Pamela.	I am 20.	He gets on well with his mother.
15	14	13	12	11	10	9	8
You don't get on well with your horse.	She is 13.	I get on well with my sister.	They get on well with his friends.	Your aunt is called Michelle.	I don't get on with your mother.	She gets on well with your dog.	You get on well with your aunt.
16	17	18	19	20	21	22	23
You (guys) get on well with your dog.	I don't get on well with your sisters.	We don't get on well with his friends.	He doesn't get on well with his sisters.	I get on well with their uncle.	You don't get on well with your cat.	You are 25.	His father is called Tristan.
FINISH	30	29	28	27	26	25	24
	Your brother is called Pierre.	I get on well with my aunt.	You don't get on well with our parents.	He is 30.	I don't get on with your brothers.	She gets on well with her parents.	You get on well with your uncle.

No Snakes No Ladders

DÉPART	**1** Je m'entends bien avec mon frère.	**2** Je ne m'entends pas bien avec ton père.	**3** Tu t'entends bien avec ton frère aîné.	**4** Tu ne t'entends pas bien avec ta sœur.	**5** Sa mère s'appelle Pamela.	**6** J'ai vingt ans.	**7** Il s'entend bien avec sa mère.
15 Tu ne t'entends pas bien avec ton cheval.	**14** Elle a treize ans.	**13** Je m'entends bien avec ma sœur.	**12** Ils s'entendent bien avec ses copains.	**11** Ta tante s'appelle Michelle.	**10** Je ne m'entends pas bien avec ta mère.	**9** Elle s'entend bien avec ton chien.	**8** Tu t'entends bien avec ta tante.
16 Vous vous entendez bien avec votre chien.	**17** Je ne m'entends pas bien avec tes sœurs.	**18** Nous ne nous entendons pas bien avec ses copains.	**19** Il ne s'entend pas bien avec ses sœurs.	**20** Je m'entends bien avec leur oncle.	**21** Tu ne t'entends pas bien avec ton chat.	**22** Tu as vingt-cinq ans.	**23** Son père s'appelle Tristan.
ARRIVÉE	**30** Ton frère s'appelle Pierre.	**29** Je m'entends bien avec ma tante.	**28** Tu ne t'entends pas bien avec nos parents.	**27** Il a trente ans.	**26** Je ne m'entends pas bien avec tes frères.	**25** Elle s'entend bien avec ses parents.	**24** Tu t'entends bien avec ton oncle.

UNIT 6 – FAST & FURIOUS – ROUND 1

1.   Bonjour. Avec qui tu __________ bien dans ta famille?
Hello. Who do you get on well with in your family?

2.   Dans ma famille, je __________ bien avec _______ parents.
In my family, I get on well with my parents.

3.   Je ____ ___________ ____ bien avec _______ sœur car elle est méchante.
I don't get on well with my sister because she is mean.

4.   Tu t'entends bien avec ____ _______?
Do you get on well with your dog?

5.   ____ ___________ _____ avec ______ profs car ils sont sympas.
He gets on well with his teachers because they are nice.

	Time 1	Time 2	Time 3	Time 4
Time				
Mistakes				

UNIT 6 – FAST & FURIOUS – ROUND 2

1.   Bonjour. Avec qui tu __________ bien dans ta famille?
Hello. Who do you get on well with in your family?

2.   Dans ma famille, je m'entends bien avec ____ _____________.
In my family, I get on well with my grandparents.

3.   Tu ____ _________ ___ bien avec ______ mère car elle est stressée.
You don't get on well with your mother because she is stressed.

4.   Tu t'entends bien avec ton __________?
Do you get on well with your cat?

5.   _____ __________ _____ avec ______ parents car ils sont gentils.
She gets on well with her parents because they are kind.

	Time 1	Time 2	Time 3	Time 4
Time				
Mistakes				

ASSESSMENT ROUND

1. Choose the correct translation (you won't need two of the sentences)

a. Tu t'entends bien avec ton frère aîné? _____

b. Je m'entends bien avec tes copains car ils sont sympas. _____

c. Tu ne t'entends pas bien avec mes frères. _____

d. Elle s'entend bien avec ses copines car elle a cinq ans. _____

e. Je ne m'entends pas bien avec ton père. _____

1. I get on well with your friends because they are nice.
2. I don't get on well with your father.
3. Do you get on well with your younger brother?
4. You don't get on well with your brothers.
5. She gets on well with her friends because she is 5.
6. Do you get on well with your older brother?
7. You don't get on well with my brothers.

2. Fill in the gaps with the missing words

a. Pendant mon temps libre, j'_________ jouer au tennis.

b. Tu t'___________ bien avec tes parents?

c. Je m'entends ____________ avec mes profs car ils sont gentils.

d. _______ chien s'appelle Benji et il a six ans.

e. Elle ne s'entend pas bien avec sa __________ car elle est impatiente.

bien	aime	mère	entends	mon

3. Translate the sentences into French

a. Who do you get on well with in your family?

b. There are four people in my family.

c. In my family, I get on well with my parents.

d. She gets on well with her mother because she is relaxed.

e. You don't get on well with your father because he is annoyed.

UNIT 7
Describing hair and eyes

Main grammar focus:

- Review of *avoir* + using adjectives in the plural form

Pop-up grammar:

- Additional practice on *avoir*

UNIT 7
Describing hair and eyes

Comment tu t'appelles? *What is your name?*			**Comment sont tes cheveux?** *What is your hair like?*
Quel âge as-tu? *How old are you?*			**De quelle couleur sont tes yeux?** *What colour are your eyes?*

Comment il/elle s'appelle? *What is his/her name?*		**Comment sont ses cheveux?** *What is his/her hair like?*
Quel âge a-t-il/elle? *How old is he/she?*		**De quelle couleur sont ses yeux?** *What colour are his/her eyes?*

Je m'appelle... *I am called* **Il/Elle s'appelle** *He/She is called*	Anthony Charles Pierre Émilie Isabelle Marie Jules Julien Robert	**et** *and*	**j'ai** *I have* **il/elle a** *he/she has*	**six ans** *6 years* **sept ans** *7 years* **huit ans** *8 years* **neuf ans** *9 years* **dix ans** *10 years* **onze ans** *11 years* **douze ans** *12 years* **treize ans** *13 years* **quatorze ans** *14 years* **quinze ans** *15 years*
J'ai les cheveux *I have...hair* **Il/Elle a les cheveux** *He/She has...hair*	**blonds** *blond* **bruns** *brown* **châtains** *light brown* **noirs** *black* **roux** *red*	**et**		**courts** *short* **en épis** *spiky* **frisés** *curly* **longs** *long* **mi-longs** *mid-length* **ondulés** *wavy* **raides** *straight* **rasés** *shaved*
J'ai les yeux *I have... eyes* **Il/Elle a les yeux** *He/She has... eyes*	**bleu<u>s</u>** *blue* **marron** *brown* **noir<u>s</u>** *black* **vert<u>s</u>** *green*	**et**	**je porte** *I wear* **il/elle porte** *he/she wears*	**des lunettes** *glasses*
			j'ai *I have* **il a** *he has*	**une moustache** *a moustache* **une barbe** *a beard*

Author's note: in the negative form in French the "des" or "une" turns into "de"
Examples: -Je **ne** porte **pas de** lunettes. *I don't wear glasses.*
          -Je **n'**ai **pas de** moustache/barbe. *I don't have a moustache/beard.*
          -Elle **ne** porte **pas de** lunettes. *She doesn't wear glasses.*
          -Il **n'**a **pas de** moustache/barbe. *He doesn't have a moustache/beard.*

MAIN GRAMMAR FOCUS
ADJECTIVES IN THE PLURAL FORM

Adjectives are used to describe a noun.

They must agree with the noun they are describing. They will be written in the masculine form or the feminine form and the singular or plural form.

When you describe your hair and your eyes, they will be in the masculine plural form. All you need to do is add an **-s** to the adjectives.

	Masculine singular	Masculine plural
blond	*blond*	*blonds*
brown	*brun*	*bruns*
light brown	*châtain*	*châtains*
black	*noir*	*noirs*
blue	*bleu*	*bleus*
green	*vert*	*verts*
short	*court*	*courts*
curly	*frisé*	*frisés*
long	*long*	*longs*
mid-length	*mi-long*	*mi-longs*
wavy	*ondulé*	*ondulés*
straight	*raide*	*raides*
shaved	*rasé*	*rasés*

However, you need to be careful with *red* and *brown*, as they do not need an **-s** in the plural form.

	Masculine singular	Masculine plural
red	*roux*	*roux*
brown	*marron*	*marron*

1. Match up

bruns	shaved
rasés	blue
mi-longs	curly
bleus	short
courts	brown
raides	straight
frisés	mid-length

2. Complete with the missing letters

a. J'ai les ch _ v _ _ x bl _ nd _ et r _ _ de _ .
I have blond and straight hair.

b. J'ai les y _ _ x v _ rt _ et m _ rr _ n.
I have green and brown eyes.

c. J'ai les _ _ eve _ x n _ ir _ et fr _ s _ s.
I have black and curly hair.

d. J'ai les _ eu _ bl _ u _ .
I have blue eyes.

3. Complete with the correct form of the adjectives

a. J'ai les cheveux ______________ et ______________ .   *I have long and brown hair.*

b. J'ai les cheveux ______________ et ______________ .   *I have short and curly hair.*

c. J'ai les cheveux ______________ et ______________ .   *I have mid-length and blond hair.*

d. J'ai les cheveux ______________ et ______________ .   *I have wavy and black hair.*

e. J'ai les cheveux ______________ et ______________ .   *I have curly and red hair.*

f. J'ai les cheveux ______________ et ______________ .   *I have wavy and light brown hair.*

g. J'ai les yeux ______________ et ______________ .   *I have green and brown eyes.*

h. J'ai les yeux ______________ et ______________ .   *I have blue and black eyes.*

4. Break the flow

a. Jailescheveuxblondsetcourts.

b. Jailesyeuxbleus.

c. Jailescheveuxbrunsetraides.

d. Jailesyeuxmarron.

e. Jailescheveuxchâtainsetfrisés.

f. Jailesyeuxnoirs.

g. Jailescheveuxrouxetmilongs.

h. Jailesyeuxverts.

5. Faulty translation: fix the English

a. J'ai les cheveux noirs et longs.
   I have black and short hair.

b. J'ai les yeux marron et verts.
   I have brown and blue eyes.

c. J'ai les cheveux châtains et mi-longs.
   She has light brown and mid-length hair.

d. J'ai les yeux noirs.
   I have black hair.

e. J'ai les cheveux roux, courts et ondulés.
   I have red, short and curly hair.

6. Choose the correct adjective	**7. Translate into French**
a. J'ai les cheveux **brun / bruns et frisé / frisés**.	a. I have brown and long hair.
b. J'ai les yeux **bleus / bleu**.	b. I have blond and short hair.
c. J'ai les cheveux **rouxs / roux et courtes / courts**.	c. I have black and curly hair.
d. J'ai les yeux **vertes / verts**.	d. I have brown eyes.
e. J'ai les cheveux **châtain / châtains**.	e. I have red and straight hair.
f. J'ai les yeux **marrons / marron**.	f. I have light brown and wavy hair.
g. J'ai les cheveux **court / courts et raides / raide**.	g. I have black and straight hair.
h. J'ai les yeux **noires / noirs**.	h. I have green and brown eyes.

POP-UP GRAMMAR
AVOIR – TO HAVE

We can use **avoir** to express a possession, a description or to say how we are feeling.

The first four parts which we will practise here are **ai**, **as** and **a**.

J'ai	*I have*	**Nous avons**	*We have*
Tu as	*You have*	**Vous avez**	*You (guys) have*
Il a	*He has*	**Ils ont**	*They (m) have*
Elle a	*She has*	**Elles ont**	*They (f) have*

8. Complete with the correct form of avoir

a. _______________ les cheveux bruns et raides.	*I have brown and straight hair.*
b. _______________ les cheveux roux et ondulés.	*She has red and wavy hair.*
c. _______________ les cheveux noirs et mi-longs.	*You have black and mid-length hair.*
d. _______________ les cheveux blonds et en épis.	*They (m) have blond and spiky hair.*
e. _______________ les yeux bleus.	*We have blue eyes.*
f. _______________ les yeux verts.	*He has green eyes.*
g. _______________ les yeux marron.	*You (guys) have brown eyes.*
h. _______________ les yeux noirs.	*They (f) have black eyes.*

9. Match up

Il a les yeux verts.	She has shaved hair.
J'ai les cheveux mi-longs et frisés.	They (m) have short and wavy hair.
Elle a les cheveux rasés.	You have brown eyes.
Tu as les yeux marron.	He has green eyes.
Vous avez les yeux noirs.	We have light brown and straight hair.
Ils ont les cheveux courts et ondulés.	You (guys) have black eyes.
Nous avons les cheveux châtains et raides.	I have mid-length and curly hair.

10. Slalom translation

J'ai	Tu as	Elle a	Ils ont	Vous avez	Il a les yeux
les yeux	les yeux verts	les yeux	les cheveux	marron	les cheveux
ondulés et	et il a	bleus et	mi-longs,	et vous avez	noirs et
les cheveux	bruns et	les cheveux	les cheveux	les cheveux	elle a les
frisés	courts	rasés	longs et noirs	yeux marron	raides

a. I have blue eyes and long and black hair.
b. You have mid-length, brown and curly hair.
c. She has wavy hair and she has brown eyes.
d. They (m) have black eyes and short hair.
e. You (guys) have green eyes and you (guys) have straight hair.
f. He has brown eyes and he has shaved hair.

11. Translate into English

a. J'ai les cheveux courts et roux.

b. Elle a les yeux verts et les cheveux longs.

c. Ils ont les cheveux courts et frisés.

d. Nous avons les yeux marron.

e. Il a les yeux bleus et les cheveux courts.

f. Tu as les cheveux blonds et ondulés.

g. Vous avez les cheveux longs, raides et noirs.

h. Elles ont les yeux verts.

12. Spot and correct the errors

a. J'ai les yeux marrons.

b. Ils ont les blonds et courts cheveux.

c. Vous avons les yeux verts.

d. Il a les cheveux longues.

e. Elles ont les cheveuxs noirs et ondulés.

f. Nous avons les bleus yeux.

g. Elle a les cheveux rouxs.

h. Tu as les cheveux courtes et frisé.

13. Choose the correct answer

a. J'ai les cheveux **courts / raides / longs**.

I have straight hair.

b. Elles ont les yeux **marron / bleus / verts**.

They have brown eyes.

c. Il a les cheveux **courts / rasés / longs**.

He has short hair.

d. Tu as les cheveux **bruns / longs / châtains**.

You have light brown hair.

e. Nous avons les cheveux **longs / blonds / frisés**.

We have blond hair.

f. Vous avez les yeux **noirs / verts / marron**.

You (guys) have green eyes.

14. Arrange the words in the correct order.

a. Comment tes sont cheveux?

What is your hair like?

b. les cheveux blonds J'ai courts et

I have short and blond hair.

c. sont tes yeux De quelle couleur?

What colour are your eyes?

d. J'ai marron bleus et les yeux

I have blue and brown eyes.

e. mi-longs les cheveux Tu as et frisés

You have mid-length and curly hair.

f. Elles ont noirs et frisés les cheveux longs,

They have long, black and curly hair.

g. les cheveux marron Elle a et les yeux courts

She has short hair and brown eyes.

h. ondulés et les cheveux Nous avons châtains

We have wavy and light brown hair.

15. Tangled translation

a. De quelle couleur sont **your eyes?**

b. J'ai les yeux **blue** et **green**.

c. Comment sont **your hair?**

d. **We have** les cheveux **mid-length** et **black**.

e. **I have** les cheveux **light brown** et **curly**.

f. **They (m) have** les yeux **brown**.

g. **She has** les cheveux **red** et **wavy**.

h. **You (guys) have** les cheveux **black** et **short**.

16. Translate into French

a. I have brown eyes.

b. He has short hair and he has blue eyes.

c. She has blond, long and curly hair.

d. They (f) have blond and wavy hair.

e. You have brown eyes and shaved hair.

f. We have wavy and black hair.

g. You (guys) have green eyes.

h. They (m) have red and wavy hair.

UNIT 7 – ORAL PING PONG – Person A

ENGLISH	FRENCH	ENGLISH	FRENCH
I have red hair.	J'ai les cheveux roux.	I have blond and short hair.	J'ai les cheveux blonds et courts.
I have brown hair.		You (guys) have light brown and long hair.	
You (guys) have brown eyes.	Vous avez les yeux marron.	He has brown and curly hair.	Il a les cheveux bruns et frisés.
I have green eyes.		She has blue eyes.	
He has grey hair.	Il a les cheveux gris.	They (m) have black and mid-length hair.	Ils ont les cheveux noirs et mi-longs.
I have blue eyes.		You have green eyes.	
We have black eyes.	Nous avons les yeux noirs.	She has brown eyes.	Elle a les yeux marron.
You have blond hair.		I have red and wavy hair.	
I have short hair.	J'ai les cheveux courts.	We have brown and straight hair.	Nous avons les cheveux bruns et raides.
They (f) have curly hair.		He has black eyes.	

UNIT 7 – ORAL PING PONG – Person B

ENGLISH	FRENCH	ENGLISH	FRENCH
I have red hair.		I have blond and short hair.	
I have brown hair.	J'ai les cheveux bruns.	You (guys) have light brown and long hair.	Vous avez les cheveux châtains et longs.
You (guys) have brown eyes.		He has brown and curly hair.	
I have green eyes.	J'ai les yeux verts.	She has blue eyes.	Elle a les yeux bleus.
He has grey hair.		They (m) have black and mid-length hair.	
I have blue eyes.	J'ai les yeux bleus.	You have green eyes.	Tu as les yeux verts.
We have black eyes.		She has brown eyes.	
You have blond hair.	Tu as les cheveux blonds.	I have red and wavy hair.	J'ai les cheveux roux et ondulés.
I have short hair.		We have brown and straight hair.	
They (f) have curly hair.	Elles ont les cheveux frisés.	He has black eyes.	Il a les yeux noirs.

No Snakes No Ladders

START

1	My name is Pierre.
2	I am 14 years old.
3	You have light brown hair.
4	She has curly hair.
5	You (guys) have brown eyes.
6	I wear glasses.
7	I have a moustache.
8	I don't have a beard.
9	Her name is Isabelle.
10	She has red hair.
11	We have wavy hair.
12	She has blue eyes.
13	She doesn't wear glasses.
14	She is 13 years old.
15	What's your name?
16	How old are you?
17	I don't get on with my sisters.
18	His name is Charles.
19	He has green eyes.
20	He has spiky hair.
21	They (m) have brown hair.
22	He is 25 years old.
23	He doesn't have a moustache.
24	He has a beard.
25	What's his name?
26	How old is she?
27	She is 30 years old.
28	I don't get on well with my parents.
29	I get on well with my aunt.
30	Your brother is called Pierre.

FINISH

No Snakes No Ladders

DÉPART

1. Je m'appelle Pierre.
2. J'ai quatorze ans.
3. Tu as les cheveux châtains.
4. Elle a les cheveux frisés.
5. Vous avez les yeux marron.
6. Je porte des lunettes.
7. J'ai une moustache.
8. Je n'ai pas de barbe.
9. Elle s'appelle Isabelle.
10. Elle a les cheveux roux.
11. Nous avons les cheveux ondulés.
12. Elle a les yeux bleus.
13. Elle ne porte pas de lunettes.
14. Elle a treize ans.
15. Comment tu t'appelles?
16. Quel âge as-tu?
17. Je ne m'entends pas bien avec mes sœurs.
18. Il s'appelle Charles.
19. Il a les yeux verts.
20. Il a les cheveux en épis.
21. Ils ont les cheveux bruns.
22. Il a vingt-cinq ans.
23. Il n'a pas de moustache.
24. Il a une barbe.
25. Comment s'appelle-t-il?
26. Quel âge a-t-elle?
27. Elle a trente ans.
28. Je ne m'entends pas bien avec mes parents.
29. Je m'entends bien avec ma tante.
30. Ton frère s'appelle Pierre.

ARRIVÉE

UNIT 7 – FAST & FURIOUS – ROUND 1

1. Bonjour. Comment tu _______________?
    Hello. What is your name?

2. Je ____________ Anthony et j'ai __________ ans.
    My name is Anthony and I am 15 years old.

3. Je ____ ____________ ____ bien avec _______ sœur car elle est méchante.
    I don't get on well with my sister because she is mean.

4. J'ai les cheveux __________, ___________ et __________.
    I have short, spiky and red hair.

5. J'ai les yeux __________ et je ____ ______ de barbe.
    I have green eyes and I don't have a beard.

	Time 1	Time 2	Time 3	Time 4
Time				
Mistakes				

UNIT 7 – FAST & FURIOUS – ROUND 2

1. Bonjour. _____________ tu t'appelles?
    Hello. What is your name?

2. Je _____________ Claire et j'ai __________ ans.
    My name is Claire and I am 13 years old.

3. Je __________________ bien avec _______ frère car il est __________.
    I get on well with my brother because he is kind.

4. J'ai les cheveux __________, ___________ et __________.
    I have long, straight and black hair.

5. J'ai les yeux __________ et je ____ __________ ____ de lunettes.
    I have brown eyes and I don't wear glasses.

	Time 1	Time 2	Time 3	Time 4
Time				
Mistakes				

ASSESSMENT ROUND

1. Choose the correct translation (you won't need two of the sentences)

a. Comment sont tes cheveux? _______

b. J'ai les cheveux courts, raides et châtains. _______

c. Il a les cheveux courts, frisés et bruns. _______

d. Elle s'entend bien avec ses copines. _______

e. J'ai une barbe mais je ne porte pas de lunettes. _______

    1.   He has short, curly and brown hair.
    2.   What's the colour of your hair?
    3.   I have short, straight and brown hair.
    4.   She gets on well with her friends.
    5.   What's your hair like?
    6.   I have a beard but I don't wear glasses.
    7.   I have short, straight and light brown hair.

2. Fill in the gaps with the missing words

a. Je m'appelle Isabelle et j'ai les _________ noirs.

b. De quelle __________ sont tes yeux?

c. J'ai les cheveux châtains, __________ et mi-longs.

d. J'ai une barbe mais je ___________ de moustache.

e. Je ne _________ pas de lunettes.

porte	n'ai pas	frisés	couleur	yeux

3. Translate the sentences into French

a. We have blond hair but my sister has black hair.

b. I have blue eyes but my brother has green eyes.

c. You (guys) have shaved hair and you (guys) have brown eyes.

d. My name is Charles and I am 18 years old.

e. I get on well with my mother because she is nice.

UNIT 8
Describing myself and another family member: physical and personality

In this unit, you will revisit:

- *Être*

- Adjectival agreement

- Possessive adjectives

- *S'entendre* (to get on/to get along)

UNIT 8
Describing myself and another family member

Combien de personnes il y a dans ta famille?	*How many people are there in your family?*
Comment est ton père/ta mère?	*What is your father/mother like?*
Tu t'entends bien avec ton frère/ta sœur?	*Do you get on well with your brother/sister?*

| Dans ma famille, il y a quatre personnes | *In my family, there are four people* |
| Il y a cinq personnes dans ma famille | *There are five people in my family* |

Dans ma famille j'ai *In my family I have…*	**mon grand-père, Claude** *my grandfather Claude* **mon père, Georges** *my father Georges* **mon oncle, Paul** *my uncle Paul* **mon petit/grand frère, Olivier** *my little/big brother Olivier* **mon cousin, Tristan** *my -boy- cousin Tristan*	**car/** **parce qu'** *because*	**il/elle est** *he/she is* **il/elle est assez** *he/she is quite*	**amusant** *fun* **beau** *handsome* **fort** *strong* **généreux** *generous* **grand** *tall* **gros** *fat* **honnête** *honest* **intelligent** *clever* **méchant** *mean* **mince** *slim* **petit** *short* **sympa** *nice* **timide** *shy* **têtu** *stubborn*
Dans ma famille il y a <u>quatre</u> personnes *There are <u>four</u> persons in my family…* **Je m'entends bien avec…** *I get along well with…* **Je m'entends mal avec…** *I get along badly with…*	**ma grand-mère, Thérèse** *my grandmother Thérèse* **ma mère, Éliane** *my mother Éliane* **ma tante, Françoise** *my aunt Françoise* **ma petite/grande sœur, Léa** *my little/big sister Léa* **ma cousine, Claire** *my -girl- cousin Claire*		**il/elle est très** *he/she is very* **il/elle est un peu** *he/she is a bit*	**amusante** *fun* **belle** *pretty* **forte** *strong* **généreuse** *generous* **grande** *tall* **grosse** *fat* **honnête** *honest* **intelligente** *clever* **méchante** *mean* **mince** *slim* **petite** *short* **sympa** *nice* **timide** *shy* **têtue** *stubborn*

1. Match up

mon frère	she is
elle est	short
fort	quite
il est	strong
petit(e)	a bit
un peu	he is
assez	my brother

2. Complete the grid

Masculine	Feminine
méchant	
	belle
	timide
gros	
amusant	
	têtue

3. Complete with the correct form of the adjective

a. Mon père est _______________ . *My father is stubborn.*

b. Ma tante est _______________ . *My aunt is tall.*

c. Il est très _______________ et _______________ . *He is very fun and clever.*

d. Elle est assez _______________ et _______________ . *She is quite mean and stubborn.*

e. Mon père est _______________ et _______________ . *My father is short and slim.*

f. Mon frère est _______________ et _______________ . *My brother is generous and nice.*

g. Ma sœur est _______________ et _______________ . *My sister is nice and short.*

h. Ma tante est _______________ et _______________ . *My aunt is pretty and clever.*

4. Translate into English

a. Comment est ton père?

b. Mon père est très grand et assez sympa.

c. Tu t'entends bien avec ton frère?

d. Elle est très sympa mais un peu timide.

e. Je m'entends bien avec ma mère.

f. Je m'entends mal avec ma grand-mère.

g. Elle est assez méchante et petite.

h. Mon petit frère est amusant.

5. Spot and correct the errors

a. Je s'entends mal avec ma cousine.

b. Elle est très têtu.

c. Elle est assez petit.

d. Je m'entends mal avec mon mère.

e. Je m'entend bien avec mon oncle.

f. Il est amusante et sympa.

g. Il est un peu méchante.

h. Il a assez honnête.

6. Choose the correct answer

a. Mon père est **amusant / sympa / généreux**.   *My father is generous.*

b. Ma mère est **petite / grande / forte**.   *My mother is tall.*

c. Je m'entends bien avec **mon oncle / ma tante / mon cousin**.   *I get on well with my aunt.*

d. Je m'entends bien avec **mon frère / ma mère / mon père**.   *I get on well with my brother.*

e. Mon cousin est **beau / mince / timide**.   *My cousin is shy.*

f. Ma cousine est **grande / intelligente / méchante**.   *My cousin is mean.*

7. Arrange the words in the correct order.

a. mon grand-père j'ai et Dans ma famille ma grand-mère.
   In my family I have my grandfather and my grandmother.

b. mon grand-père Je m'entends bien avec car très sympa il est.
   I get on well with my grandfather because he is very nice.

c. avec ma grand-mère Je m'entends mal car assez elle est têtue.
   I get along badly with my grandmother because she is quite stubborn.

d. amusante est assez Ma petite sœur mais méchante un peu.
   My little sister is quite fun but a bit mean.

e. très est généreux Mon grand frère un peu mais timide.
   My big brother is very generous but a bit shy.

f. très fort Mon père très grand est et.
   My father is very tall and very strong.

8. Choose the correct translation

a.	**I get on well**	je m'entends bien	je m'entends mal	je ne supporte pas
b.	**I get on badly**	je m'entends bien	je m'entends mal	je ne supporte pas
c.	**he is nice**	il est gentil	il est sympa	il est génial
d.	**she is strong**	elle est petite	elle est grande	elle est forte
e.	**he is fun**	il est drôle	il est amusant	il est marrant
f.	**she is short**	elle est petite	elle est minuscule	elle est grande
g.	**he is handsome**	il est moche	il est petit	il est beau
h.	**she is pretty**	elle est grande	elle est belle	elle est sympa

9. Slalom translation

Je m'entends	Mon père	Ma mère	Je m'entends	Mon cousin	Mon chat
est très	est assez	bien avec	est un peu	mal avec	est
petit	ma sœur	honnête	mon frère	très grand	forte
mais un peu	et assez	et un peu	car elle est	mais assez	car il est
têtu	méchant	gros	généreuse	amusante	timide

a. I get on well with my sister because she is fun.

b. My father is very tall and quite stubborn.

c. My mother is very strong and a bit generous.

d. I get along badly with my brother because he is mean.

e. My cousin (m) is quite honest but a bit shy.

f. My cat is a bit short but quite fat.

---

10. Guided translation: complete the translation

a. I get along well with my father.   Je m' ______________ bien avec ________ père.

b. I get along badly with my cousin. (f)   Je m' ______________ mal avec ________ cousine.

c. He is very short but strong.   Il est très _________ mais ___________ .

d. She is clever but quite mean.   Elle est ______________ mais assez ___________ .

e. My dog is very handsome.   Mon chien est vraiment ___________ .

f. My cat is quite slim.   Mon chat _________ assez ___________ .

---

11. Tangled translation

a. Dans ma famille, j'ai **my grandfather.**

b. **I get on well with** ma tante.

c. Elle est un peu **clever.**

d. **I get on badly with** ma cousine.

e. **She is** assez **tall** et un peu **pretty.**

f. **He is** assez **stubborn.**

g. **My big sister** est très **nice.**

h. **My little brother** est un peu **strong.**

12. Translate into French

a. My cousin (m) is mean.

b. My cat is very fat.

c. My sister is a bit honest.

d. My mother is very clever.

e. My uncle is a bit fun.

f. My cousin (f) is quite pretty.

g. My aunt is very tall.

h. My grandfather is quite stubborn.

No Snakes No Ladders

START	**1** I get along well with my grandfather.	**2** He is very tall.	**3** I get along badly with my mother.	**4** She is quite stubborn.	**5** He is a bit mean.	**6** I get along badly with my cousin (m).	**7** He is very short.
15 He is very slim.	**14** She is a bit strong.	**13** I get along badly with my aunt.	**12** She is quite clever.	**11** He is a bit nice.	**10** I get along well with my brother.	**9** I get along well with my mother.	**8** He is a bit generous.
16 I get along well with my cousin (f).	**17** She is a bit tall.	**18** I get along well with my father.	**19** He is a bit slim.	**20** She is quite shy.	**21** He is very handsome.	**22** She is a bit short.	**23** He is very nice.
FINISH	**30** I get along badly with my sister.	**29** She is quite fun.	**28** I get along badly with my parents.	**27** I get along well with my uncle.	**26** She is quite honest.	**25** He is very clever.	**24** She is quite mean.

No Snakes No Ladders

	1	2	3	4	5	6	7
DÉPART	Je m'entends bien avec mon grand-père.	Il est très grand.	Je m'entends mal avec ma mère.	Elle est assez têtue.	Il est un peu méchant.	Je m'entends mal avec mon cousin.	Il est très petit.
15 Il est très mince.	**14** Elle est un peu forte.	**13** Je m'entends mal avec ma tante.	**12** Elle est assez intelligente.	**11** Il est un peu sympa.	**10** Je m'entends bien avec mon frère.	**9** Je m'entends bien avec ma mère.	**8** Il est un peu généreux.
16 Je m'entends bien avec ma cousine.	**17** Elle est un peu grande.	**18** Je m'entends bien avec mon père.	**19** Il est un peu mince.	**20** Elle est assez timide.	**21** Il est très beau.	**22** Elle est un peu petite.	**23** Il est très sympa.
ARRIVÉE	**30** Je m'entends mal avec ma sœur.	**29** Elle est assez amusante.	**28** Je m'entends mal avec mes parents.	**27** Je m'entends bien avec mon oncle.	**26** Elle est assez honnête.	**25** Il est très intelligent.	**24** Elle est assez méchante.

UNIT 8 – FAST & FURIOUS – ROUND 1

1. Bonjour. Comment est _______ __________?
   Hello. What is your father like?

2. Mon père est très __________, __________ et __________.
   My father is very tall, strong and nice.

3. Tu ___ _____________ bien avec _____ mère?
   Do you get on well with your mother?

4. Je ___ _____________ bien avec _____ mère.
   I get on well with my mother.

5. Elle est très __________, __________ et __________.
   She is very fun, intelligent and honest.

	Time 1	Time 2	Time 3	Time 4
Time				
Mistakes				

UNIT 8 – FAST & FURIOUS – ROUND 2

1. Bonjour. Comment est _______ __________?
   Hello. What is your brother like?

2. Mon frère est très __________, __________ et __________.
   My father is very handsome, generous and slim.

3. Tu ___ _____________ bien avec _____ sœur?
   Do you get on well with your sister?

4. Je ___ _____________ mal avec _____ sœur.
   I get along badly with my sister.

5. Elle est très __________, __________ et __________.
   She is very stubborn, mean and short.

	Time 1	Time 2	Time 3	Time 4
Time				
Mistakes				

ASSESSMENT ROUND

1. Choose the correct translation (you won't need two of the sentences)

a. Tu t'entends bien avec ton frère? _____

b. Je m'entends mal avec mon oncle. _____

c. Il est très grand, assez amusant et intelligent. _____

d. Je m'entends mal avec ma sœur. _____

e. Elle est assez forte, méchante et têtue. _____

    1.   I get along badly with my sister.
    2.   He is very tall, quite fun and clever.
    3.   She is a bit strong, mean and stubborn.
    4.   Do you get on well with your brother?
    5.   She is quite strong, mean and stubborn.
    6.   I get along badly with my uncle.
    7.   He is quite tall, very fun and clever.

2. Fill in the gaps with the missing words

a. Je m'appelle Isabelle et j'ai __________ ans.

b. Je m' __________ bien avec ma mère.

c. Elle est très __________ et généreuse.

d. Je m'entends mal avec __________ père.

e. Il est assez __________ et méchant.

sympa	treize	têtu	entends	mon

3. Translate the sentences into French

a. I get along well with my grandmother.

b. My big brother is very nice, quite honest and generous.

c. She is a bit pretty, short and generous.

d. Do you get on well with your grandfather?

e. She is quite fun, strong and clever.

UNIT 9
Comparing people's appearance and personality

Main grammar focus:

- To use comparatives
  (*plus...que, moins...que, aussi...que*)

Pop-up grammar:

- Review of adjectival agreement

UNIT 9
Comparing people

Elle			affectueux/euse(s) *affectionate*	ma grand-mère
Il			aimable(s) *likeable*	mon grand-père
Ma grand-mère			amusant(e)(s) *funny*	mon amie <u>Anne</u>
Mon grand-père			antipathique(s) *unfriendly*	mon ami <u>Paul</u>
Mon amie <u>Anne</u>			barbant(e)(s) *boring*	mon chat
Mon ami <u>Paul</u>			bavard(e)(s) *talkative*	ma sœur
Mon chat			beau(x)/belle(s)	mon frère
Ma sœur			*good-looking*	mon fils
Mon frère		**plus**	bruyant(e)(s) *noisy*	ma fille
Mon fils *son*		*more*	faible(s) *weak*	ma mère
Ma fille *daughter*			fort(e)(s) *strong*	ma meilleure amie
Ma mère			grand(e)(s) *tall*	mon meilleur ami
Ma meilleure amie	**est**		gros/se(s) *fat*	mon père
Mon meilleur ami	*is*	**moins**	intelligent(e)(s) *intelligent*	mon canard
Mon père		*less*	jeune(s) *young*	mon chien
Mon canard	**sont**		mince(s) *slim*	ma cousine
Mon chien	*are*		moche(s) *ugly*	mon cousin
Ma cousine		**aussi**	paresseux/euse(s) *lazy*	ma tortue
Mon cousin		*as*	petit(e)(s) *short*	ma tante
Ma tortue			sérieux/euse(s) *serious*	mon oncle
Ma tante			sportif/ive(s) *sporty*	mes grands-parents
Mon oncle			stupide(s) *stupid*	mes sœurs
Mes grands-parents			sympa *nice*	mes frères
Mes sœurs			tranquille(s) *relaxed*	ma petite amie *gf*
Mes frères			travailleur/euse(s) *hard-working*	mon petit ami *bf*
Ma petite amie *gf*			vieux/vieille(s) *old*	mes parents
Mon petit ami *bf*				mes oncles
Mes parents				moi
Mes oncles				

(With **que** / *than / as* before the right-hand column.)

MAIN GRAMMAR FOCUS
COMPARATIVES

In French, to say *more...than,* we use **plus...que**

> **Mon frère est plus sportif que mon père.**
> *My brother is more sporty than my father.*

In French, to say *less...than,* we use **moins...que**

> **Mes frères sont moins grands que mon père.**
> *My brothers are less tall than my father.*

In French, to say *as...as,* we use **aussi...que**

> **Mon frère est aussi sympa que mon père.**
> *My brother is as nice as my father.*

The adjective must agree with the noun it is referring to:

> **Mon père est plus fort que ma mère.**
> *My father is stronger than my mother.*
> **Ma grandmère est plus fortE que mon grand-père.**
> *My grandmother is stronger than my grandfather.*

There are some adjectives that are exceptions when used as a comparative:

> **pire que**   *worse than*
> **meilleur que**   *better than*

1. Match up	

plus grand que	stronger than
plus fort que	as weak as
moins sympa que	less old than
moins vieux que	taller than
aussi petit que	younger than
aussi faible que	less nice than
plus jeune que	as short as

2. Complete with the missing letters

a. Il est pl _ s b _ v _ rd q _ _ mon père.
He is more talkative than my father.

b. Elle est m _ _ ns sp _ rt _ v _ q _ _ m _ _ .
She is less sporty than me.

c. Ils sont pl _ s b _ _ _ x q _ _ mes frères.
They are more good-looking than my brothers.

d. Elles sont m _ _ ns p _ t _ t _ s q _ _ toi.
They are less short than you.

3. Complete with the correct form of the adjective

a. Elle est plus ___________ que mon frère. — *She is taller than my brother.*

b. Il est moins ___________ que mon père. — *He is less serious than my father.*

c. Ils sont plus ___________ que leur sœur. — *They are shorter than their sister.*

d. Nous sommes aussi ___________ que notre mère. — *We are as talkative as our mother.*

e. Mon père est moins ___________ que mon oncle. — *My father is less strong than my uncle.*

f. Mes frères sont aussi ___________ que mes amis. — *My brothers are as lazy as my friends.*

g. Vous êtes plus ___________ que votre mère. — *You (guys) are sportier than your mother.*

h. Ma tante est moins ___________ que ma cousine. — *My aunt is less boring than my cousin.*

4. Break the flow

a. Leurfilsestplusfortquemoncousin.

b. Noussommesplussympasqueleursœur.

c. Matortueestplusstupidequemonchien.

d. Monchatestmoinsgrosquemoncanard.

e. Mamèreestaussibavardequemoi.

f. Monpèreestaussibruyantquemonfrère.

g. Vousêtesmoinsgrandesquemononcle.

h. Mesfrèressontmoinssportifsquemoi.

5. Faulty translation: fix the English

a. Ma fille est plus aimable que mon fils.
   My son is more likeable than my daughter.

b. Leur ami est plus petit que mon frère.
   Their friend is taller than my brother.

c. Mon chat est plus stupide que ma tortue.
   My cat is less stupid than my turtle.

d. Il est aussi paresseux que moi.
   He is less lazy than me.

e. Elle sont moins sérieuses que leur mère.
   They are as serious as their mother.

<table>
<tr><td>

6. Choose the correct adjective

a. Votre sœur est moins **bavard / bavarde** que moi.

b. Mon frère est plus **sportif / sportive** que toi.

c. Ton chat est plus **petit / petite** que mon chien.

d. Mes parents sont plus **vieux / vieilles** que moi.

e. Ma tortue est aussi **beau / belle** que ton chat.

f. Il est moins **travailleur / travailleuse** que moi.

g. Elle est plus **grand / grande** que ma cousine.

h. Il est aussi **amusant / amusante** que mon fils.

</td><td>

7. Translate into French

a. He is as affectionate as me.

b. She is as noisy as her uncle.

c. He is less weak than my brother.

d. She is more relaxed than me.

e. He is more talkative than me.

f. She is less tall than her sister.

g. He is as strong as my friend.

h. She is less likeable than me.

</td></tr>
</table>

POP-UP GRAMMAR
ADJECTIVES

Adjectives are used to describe a noun.

They must agree with the noun they are describing. They will be written in the masculine form or the feminine form.

If the adjective ends with **-eur** in the masculine form, it will change to **-euse** in the feminine form:

Il est travailleur.
He is hard-working.

Elle est travaill<u>euse</u>.
She is hard-working.

If the adjective ends with **-if** in the masculine form, it will change to **-ive** in the feminine form:

Il est sportif.
He is sporty.

Elle est sport<u>ive</u>.
She is sporty.

The adjective **gros** will double the final consonant in the feminine form:

Le chat est gros.
The cat is fat.

La tortue est gros<u>se</u>.
The turtle is fat.

The adjective **sympa** will stay the same in the masculine and the feminine form:

Il est sympa. *He is nice.*   **Elle est sympa.** *She is nice.*

8. Match up

Elle est plus intelligente que moi	She is as boring as my sister
Il est moins beau que mon petit ami	She is less lazy than me
Elle est aussi barbante que ma sœur	You (guys) are funnier than our friends
Il est plus mince que ton chien	He is less good-looking than my boyfriend
Elle est moins paresseuse que moi	They are as short as their brother
Ils sont aussi petits que leur frère	She is more intelligent than me
Vous êtes plus amusantes que nos amies	He is slimmer than your dog

9. Slalom translation

Mon père	Mes amis	Mon canard	Nous	Vous êtes	Mes chiens
moins	est aussi	sont plus	est plus	sont aussi	sommes plus
gros	jeunes	travailleurs	moches	bavardes	grand
que votre	que ma	que mes	que mes	que vos	que mon
chat	parents	frères	chats	mère	sœur

a. My father is taller than my mother.

b. My friends are more hard-working than my brothers.

c. My duck is as fat as my cat.

d. We are younger than your parents.

e. You (guys) are less talkative than your sister.

f. My dogs are as ugly as my cats.

10. Translate into English

a. Il est moins affecteux que son frère.

b. Mon chat est aussi moche que son chien.

c. Ma tortue est plus stupide que ton chat.

d. Ma mère est plus jeune que ma tante.

e. Mon ami est plus vieux que mon frère.

f. Mes amies sont plus belles que vos amis.

g. Mes sœurs sont plus drôles que moi.

h. Mon petit frère est plus amusant que toi.

11. Spot and correct the errors

a. Mon canard est plu moche que mon chat.

b. Elle est moins intelligent que sa sœur.

c. Il est que amusant aussi mon père.

d. Elle est plus que bruyante mes amis.

e. Mes oncles sont plu faible que mes tantes.

f. Il est moins amusante que ma mère.

g. Il est plus sportive que ma sœur.

h. Mes amis sont moins petit que moi.

12. Choose the correct answer

a. Mon père est plus **amusant / sympa / généreux**.　　　*My father is nicer.*

b. Ma mère est plus **petite / grande / forte**.　　　*My mother is stronger.*

c. Mes parents sont moins **sportifs / sérieux / barbants**.　　　*My parents are less boring.*

d. Nos amis sont plus **jeunes / bruyants / tranquilles**.　　　*Our friends are noisier.*

e. Vos canards sont plus **beaux / minces / timides**.　　　*Your ducks are slimmer.*

f. Leur tortue est plus **grande / intelligente / moche**.　　　*Their turtle is uglier.*

---

13. Arrange the words in the correct order.

a. est moins Ta grand-mère que ta mère antipathique
   Your grandmother is less unfriendly than your mother.

b. est aussi beau Mon ami Paul que mon ami Pierre
   My friend Paul is as handsome as my friend Pierre.

c. Leur chat que est plus gros leur chien
   Their cat is fatter than their dog.

d. que ton frère est plus amusante Ma petite sœur
   My little sister is more fun than your brother.

e. est plus généreux que Mon grand frère mon petit frère
   My older brother is more generous than my younger brother.

---

14. Tangled translation

a. **Their** chat est **as fat as** mon chien.

b. Sa tortue est **slimmer than** mon canard.

c. Elle est **more intelligent than** ma sœur.

d. Ma cousine est **less sporty than** moi.

e. **She is** aussi **tall** que mon amie.

f. **He is less** bavard que **my father.**

g. **They (f) are nicer than** ton amie.

h. **My little brother** est **stronger than** toi.

15. Translate into French

a. My cat is as slim as my dog.

b. Your girlfriend is taller than my sister.

c. Their parents are older than your parents.

d. My mother is as clever as my father.

e. Your uncles are funnier than your aunts.

f. My cousin (f) is lazier than my brother.

g. My turtle is less stupid than his duck.

h. My grandfather is as sporty as me.

UNIT 9 – ORAL PING PONG – Person A

ENGLISH	FRENCH	ENGLISH	FRENCH
Your father is shorter than my grandfather.	Ton père est plus petit que mon grand-père.	**My friend Anne is less talktative than me.**	Mon amie Anne est moins bavarde que moi.
My sister is less sporty than me.		**My best friend (f) is as nice as my sister.**	
Her son is as strong as his daughter.	Son fils est aussi fort que sa fille.	**You are more boring (f) than my brother.**	Tu es plus barbante que mon frère.
My cat is fatter than my dog.		**Their parents are less hard-working than her grandparents.**	
Your dogs are less lazy than your cats.	Tes chiens sont moins paresseux que tes chats.	**My sisters are as unfriendly as my brothers.**	Mes sœurs sont aussi antipathiques que mes frères.
My uncle is as serious as my aunt.		**My girlfriend is more intelligent than me.**	
Their brother is more likeable than me.	Leur frère est plus aimable que moi.	**We are less funny than your best friend (m).**	Nous sommes moins amusants que ton meilleur ami.
My grandmother is less relaxed than my mother.		**My uncle is older than my father.**	
My cousin (m) is as noisy as my brother.	Mon cousin est aussi bruyant que mon frère.	**They (m) are sportier than my brothers.**	Ils sont plus sportifs que mes frères.
My turtle is uglier than my duck.		**My friend Paul is less boring than my friend Antoine.**	

UNIT 9 – ORAL PING PONG – Person B

ENGLISH	FRENCH	ENGLISH	FRENCH
Your father is shorter than my grandfather.		My friend Anne is less talktative than me.	
My sister is less sporty than me.	Ma sœur est moins sportive que moi.	My best friend (f) is as nice as my sister.	Ma meilleure amie est aussi sympa que ma sœur.
Her son is as strong as his daughter.		You are more boring (f) than my brother.	
My cat is fatter than my dog.	Mon chat est plus gros que mon chien.	Their parents are less hard-working than her grandparents.	Leurs parents sont moins travailleurs que ses grands-parents.
Your dogs are less lazy than your cats.		My sisters are as unfriendly as my brothers.	
My uncle is as serious as my aunt.	Mon oncle est aussi sérieux que ma tante.	My girlfriend is more intelligent than me.	Ma petite amie est plus intelligente que moi.
Their brother is more likeable than me.		We are less funny than your best friend (m).	
My grandmother is less relaxed than my mother.	Ma grand-mère est moins tranquille que ma mère.	My uncle is older than my father.	Mon oncle est plus vieux que mon père.
My cousin (m) is as noisy as my brother.		They (m) are sportier than my brothers.	
My turtle is uglier than my duck.	Ma tortue est plus moche que mon canard.	My friend Paul is less boring than my friend Antoine.	Mon ami Paul est moins barbant que mon ami Antoine.

No Snakes No Ladders

1 — She is more serious than my sister.

2 — He is less tall than my brother.

3 — She is as noisy as my daughter.

4 — He is as young as my uncle.

5 — He is as nice as my father.

6 — She is less relaxed than me.

7 — He is older than my aunt.

8 — She is more relaxed.

9 — My duck is as stupid as my dog.

10 — They (f) are less sporty than me.

11 — He is less serious than my mother.

12 — She is shorter than my aunt.

13 — He is less lazy than my friend.

14 — She is stronger than her cat.

15 — My cat is slimmer than my dog.

START

16 — She is more affectionate.

17 — They are less likeable.

18 — He is funnier than my cousin.

19 — They (f) are more boring.

20 — She is as talkative as my friend.

21 — He is more handsome than my duck.

22 — She is weaker than my friend.

23 — I am taller (m) than my son.

24 — She is as young as my daughter.

25 — He is less clever than my uncle.

26 — She is more honest than my mother.

27 — She is younger than my uncle.

28 — My parents are as nice as my brothers.

29 — We are lazier (m) than our aunts.

30 — My brothers are as strong as my sisters.

FINISH

No Snakes No Ladders

DÉPART

1. Elle est plus sérieuse que ma sœur.
2. Il est moins grand que mon frère.
3. Elle est aussi bruyante que ma fille.
4. Il est aussi jeune que mon oncle.
5. Il est aussi sympa que mon père.
6. Elle est moins tranquille que moi.
7. Il est plus vieux que ma tante.
8. Elle est plus tranquille.
9. Mon canard est aussi stupide que mon chien.
10. Elles sont moins sportives que moi.
11. Il est moins sérieux que ma mère.
12. Elle est plus petite que ma tante.
13. Il est moins paresseux que mon ami.
14. Elle est plus forte que son chat.
15. Mon chat est plus mince que mon chien.
16. Elle est plus affectueuse.
17. Ils sont moins aimables.
18. Il est plus amusant que mon cousin.
19. Elles sont plus barbantes.
20. Elle est aussi bavarde que mon ami.
21. Il est plus beau que mon canard.
22. Elle est plus faible que mon ami.
23. Je suis plus grand que mon fils.
24. Elle est aussi jeune que ma fille.
25. Il est moins intelligent que mon oncle.
26. Elle est moins honnête que ma mère.
27. Elle est plus jeune que mon oncle.
28. Mes parents sont aussi sympa que mes frères.
29. Nous sommes plus paresseux que nos tantes.
30. Mes frères sont plus forts que mes sœurs.

ARRIVÉE

114

UNIT 9 – FAST & FURIOUS – ROUND 1

1. Bonjour. Comment est _______ __________?
   Hello. What is your father like?

2. Mon père est plus __________ que ma mère mais ________ petit ________ mon oncle.
   My father is older than my mother but shorter than my uncle.

3. Tu t'____________ bien avec ta ________?
   Do you get on well with your mother?

4. Non car elle est ________ ________ ________ ma tante.
   No, because she is less nice than my aunt.

5. Mon chien est ________ ________ ________ mon chat.
   My dog is as fat as my cat.

	Time 1	Time 2	Time 3	Time 4
Time				
Mistakes				

UNIT 9 – FAST & FURIOUS – ROUND 2

1. Bonjour. Comment est _______ __________?
   Hello. What is your brother like?

2. Mon frère est plus __________ que ma sœur mais ________ jeune ________ moi.
   My brother is nicer than my sister but younger than me.

3. Tu t'____________ bien avec ta ________?
   Do you get on well with your aunt?

4. Non car elle est ________ ________ ________ ma mère.
   No because she is less funny than my mother.

5. Mon canard est ________ ______________ ________ ma tortue.
   My dog is as lazy as my turtle.

	Time 1	Time 2	Time 3	Time 4
Time				
Mistakes				

ASSESSMENT ROUND

1. Choose the correct translation (you won't need two of the sentences)

a. Ma grand-mère est plus sympa que mon grand-père. _____

b. Ma cousine est moins paresseuse que mon cousin. _____

c. Mon fils est moins grand que ma fille. _____

d. Mon oncle est aussi intelligent que ma mère. _____

e. Mon chien est moins vieux que mon canard. _____

1. My son is less tall than my daughter.
2. My uncle is more intelligent than my mother.
3. My grandmother is nicer than my grandfather.
4. My uncle is as intelligent as my mother.
5. My dog is less old than my duck.
6. My (girl) cousin is less lazy than my (boy) cousin.
7. My son is shorter than my daughter.

2. Fill in the gaps with the missing words

a. Je m'appelle Isabelle et j'ai __________ ans.

b. Je m' ___________ bien avec ma mère.

c. Elle est plus _______________ que mon père.

d. Mon père est __________ affectueux que ma mère.

e. Mes parents sont aussi ___________ que mes oncles.

sportifs	quinze	moins	entends	généreuse

3. Translate the sentences into French

a. I get along well with my parents.

b. My big brother is nicer than my little brother.

c. She is less generous than me.

d. Their dog is more intelligent than my duck.

e. Her aunt is as strong as her uncle.

UNIT 10 – Describing my teachers and saying why I like them

In this unit you will revisit:

- *Être*

- Adjectival agreements

- -ER verbs: *adorer* and *aimer*

Unit 10
Describing my teachers and saying why I like them

Quel(le) professeur(e) tu (n') aimes (pas)? Pourquoi? *Which teacher do you (not) like? Why?*					
Tu aimes ton/ta professeur(e) de dessin? Pourquoi? *Do you like your art teacher? Why?*					

J'adore *I love* **J'aime** *I like* **Je n'aime pas** *I don't like*	**mon professeur** *my teacher (m)* **ma professeure** *my teacher (f)*	**d'**	allemand anglais éducation physique espagnol histoire informatique		**ennuyeux** *boring* **gentil** *kind* **impatient** *impatient* **intelligent** *intelligent* **intéressant** *interesting* **méchant** *mean* **patient** *patient* **strict** *strict* **travailleur** *hard-working*
Il/Elle adore *He/she loves* **Il/Elle aime** *He/she likes*	**son professeur** *his/her teacher (m)* **sa professeure** *his/her teacher (f)*			**parce qu' il/elle est** *because he/she is*	
Nous adorons *We love* **Nous aimons** *We like*	**notre professeur** *our teacher (m)* **notre professeure** *our teacher (f)*	**de**	dessin français mathématiques musique sciences technologie théâtre	**parce qu' il/elle n'est pas** *because he/she is not*	**drôle** *funny* **sympathique** *nice*
Vous adorez *You guys love* **Vous aimez** *You guys like*	**votre professeur** *your teacher (m)* **votre professeure** *your teacher (f)*				**ennuyeuse** **gentille** **impatiente** **intéressante** **méchante** **patiente** **stricte** **travailleuse**
Ils/Elles adorent *They love* **Ils/Elles aiment** *They like*	**leur professeur** *their teacher (m)* **leur professeure** *their teacher (f)*				

<table>
<tr><td colspan="2">

1. Match up

</td><td colspan="2">

2. Complete the grid

</td></tr>
</table>

<table>
<tr><td>

j'adore

</td><td>they don't like</td></tr>
<tr><td>

nous aimons

</td><td>you aren't</td></tr>
<tr><td>

ils n'aiment pas

</td><td>he is never</td></tr>
<tr><td>

il n'est jamais

</td><td>I love</td></tr>
<tr><td>

vous êtes

</td><td>I am</td></tr>
<tr><td>

tu n'es pas

</td><td>you (guys) are</td></tr>
<tr><td>

je suis

</td><td>we like</td></tr>
</table>

Masculine	Feminine
ennuyeux	
	impatiente
	travailleuse
gentil	
	intelligente
strict	

3. Complete with the correct form of the adjective

a. Nous aimons notre prof parce qu'il est __________ . *We like our teacher because he is kind.*

b. J'adore ma prof parce qu'elle est ______________ . *I love my teacher because she is patient.*

c. Ils aiment leur prof parce qu'il est ______________ . *They like their teacher because he is funny.*

d. Il adore son prof parce qu'il est ______________ . *He loves his teacher because he is nice.*

e. J'adore ma prof parce qu'elle est ______________ . *I love my teacher because she is interesting.*

f. Je n'aime pas mon prof car il est ______________ . *I don't like my teacher because he is mean.*

g. Je n'aime pas ma prof car elle est ______________ . *I don't like my teacher because she is strict.*

4. Translate into English

a. J'adore ma prof de dessin…

b. …parce qu'elle est gentille.

c. Vous n'aimez pas votre prof de français…

d. …parce qu'il n'est jamais patient.

e. Elles aiment leur prof d'espagnol…

f. …parce qu'il est travailleur.

g. Tu n'aimes pas ta prof de sciences…

h. …parce qu'elle est impatiente.

5. Spot and correct the errors

a. J'aimes mon prof de musique…

b. …parce qu'il est patiente.

c. Ils naimes pas leur prof de technologie…

d. …parce qu'elle est méchant.

e. Nous adorez notre prof de mathématiques…

f. …parce qu'elle ne est jamais en colère.

g. Vous aimons votre prof de théâtre…

h. …parce qu'elle n'est pas ennuyeux.

6. Choose the correct answer

a. Mon prof n'est pas **ennuyeux / impatient / strict**. *My teacher isn't boring.*

b. Sa prof est **gentille / intéressante / drôle**. *His/Her teacher is funny.*

c. Ton prof est **intelligent / patient / travailleur**. *Your teacher is patient.*

d. Notre prof n'est pas **stricte / ennuyeuse / méchante**. *Our teacher (f) isn't mean.*

e. Votre prof est **intelligent / patient / gentil**. *Your teacher is kind.*

f. Ma prof est **impatiente / sympathique / travailleuse**. *My teacher is hard-working.*

---

7. Arrange the words in the correct order.

a. mon prof de dessin J'aime gentil parce qu'il est
I like my art teacher because he is kind.

b. sa prof d'allemand Elle n'aime pas parce qu' méchante elle est
She doesn't like her German teacher because she is mean.

c. ta prof travailleuse de français parce qu'elle est Tu adores
You love your French teacher because she is hard-working.

d. parce qu'il Vous aimez n'est jamais votre prof d'espagnol strict
You (guys) like your Spanish teacher because he is never strict.

e. notre prof Nous adorons de jamais théâtre impatient parce qu'il n'est
We love our drama teacher because he is never impatient.

f. intelligente Ils n'aiment pas parce qu'elle leur prof de sciences n'est pas
They don't like their science teacher because she is not intelligent.

---

8. Choose the correct translation

a.	**he likes**	elle aime	il aime	tu aimes
b.	**we love**	nous adorons	il adore	elle adore
c.	**never**	pas	plus	jamais
d.	**they are**	tu es	je suis	ils sont
e.	**you like**	elle aime	il aime	tu aimes
f.	**you (guys) are**	tu es	vous êtes	il est
g.	**they love**	j'adore	tu adores	elles adorent
h.	**she is**	il est	elle est	tu es

9. Slalom translation

Tu aimes	Ils adorent	Il n'aime pas	Je n'aime pas	Vous adorez	Nous aimons
sa prof de	votre prof de	ta prof d'	mon prof de	leur prof d'	notre prof de
théâtre	anglais	musique	histoire	sciences	maths
parce qu'il	parce qu'elle	parce qu'elle	parce qu'elle	parce qu'il	parce qu'il
est drôle	est gentil	est stricte	est sympa	est patient	est gentille

a. You like your English teacher because she is kind.

b. They love their history teacher because he is patient.

c. He doesn't like his maths teacher because she is strict.

d. I don't like my music teacher because he is funny.

e. You (guys) love your science teacher because she is nice.

f. We like our drama teacher because he is kind.

10. Guided translation: complete the translation

a. My French teacher is never mean.   Mon _______ de français __'est ______ méchant.

b. Our IT teacher is hard-working (f).   Notre prof d'informatique _____ _____________ .

c. Your science teacher is not funny.   Ta prof de _________ __'est ______ drôle.

d. My Spanish teacher is kind.   Ma prof d'____________ est ___________ .

e. Their drama teacher is interesting (m).   Leur prof de _________ est ____________ .

f. They love their German teacher.   Ils ___________ leur ______________ d'allemand.

11. Tangled translation

a. J'**love** ma prof d'**English**…

b. …parce qu'elle est **nice.**

c. Il n'aime pas son **teacher** de français…

d. …parce qu'il n'est **never funny.**

e. Vous **like** votre prof d'**Spanish**…

f. …parce qu'il est **intelligent.**

g. Elles n'aiment **not** leur prof de sciences…

h. …parce qu'**she is mean.**

12. Translate into French

a. I like my German teacher…

b. …because he is hard-working.

c. He loves his drama teacher…

d. …because she is funny.

e. We don't like our maths teacher…

f. …because she is never patient.

g. They (m) like their history teacher…

h. …because he is intelligent.

No Snakes No Ladders

START	**1** I love…	**2** They (m) like…	**3** I don't like…	**4** We are boring.	**5** She is kind.	**6** You (guys) are impatient.	**7** She is intelligent.
15 She is not impatient.	**14** He is not kind.	**13** She is not boring.	**12** They (m) are hard-working.	**11** They (f) are strict.	**10** You (guys) are patient (f).	**9** She is mean.	**8** You are interesting.
16 He is not intelligent.	**17** You are not interesting (f).	**18** He is not mean.	**19** She is not patient.	**20** They (m) are not strict.	**21** She is not hard-working.	**22** She is always in a good mood.	**23** He is never in a good mood.
FINISH	**30** You are not boring (m).	**29** You are mean and strict (m).	**28** We are patient and kind (f).	**27** She is always angry.	**26** He is always angry.	**25** She is never in a bad mood.	**24** He is always in a bad mood.

No Snakes No Ladders

DÉPART

1 J'adore...	**2** Ils aiment...	**3** Je n'aime pas...	**4** Nous sommes ennuyeux.	**5** Elle est gentille.	**6** Vous êtes impatients.	**7** Elle est intelligente.
14 Il n'est pas gentil.	**13** Elle n'est pas ennuyeuse.	**12** Ils sont travailleurs.	**11** Elles sont strictes.	**10** Vous êtes patientes.	**9** Elle est méchante.	**8** Tu es intéressant.
15 Elle n'est pas impatiente.	**18** Il n'est pas méchant.	**19** Elle n'est pas patiente.	**20** Ils ne sont pas stricts.	**21** Elle n'est pas travailleuse.	**22** Elle est toujours de bonne humeur.	**23** Il n'est jamais de bonne humeur.
16 Il n'est pas intelligent.	**17** Tu n'es pas intéressante.	**28** Nous sommes patientes et gentilles.	**27** Elle est toujours en colère.	**26** Il est toujours en colère.	**25** Elle n'est jamais de mauvaise humeur.	**24** Il est toujours de mauvaise humeur.
ARRIVÉE	**30** Vous n'êtes pas ennuyeux.	**29** Tu es méchant et strict.				

UNIT 10 – FAST & FURIOUS – ROUND 1

1. Bonjour. Tu ______ ton _________ de dessin?
   Hello. Do you like your art teacher?

2. Oui, _________ mon prof de _________ parce qu'il est _________.
   Yes, I like my art teacher because he is hard-working.

3. Tu ________ ta prof de mathématiques?
   Do you like your maths teacher?

4. Non, je __________ _____ ma prof de mathématiques ________ ____'elle n'est pas ______.
   No, I don't like my maths teacher because she is not patient.

5. J'________ mon prof de français parce qu'____ _______ _________ de mauvaise humeur.
   I love my French teacher because he is never in a bad mood.

	Time 1	Time 2	Time 3	Time 4
Time				
Mistakes				

UNIT 10 – FAST & FURIOUS – ROUND 2

1. Bonjour. Tu ______ ton _________ de théâtre?
   Hello. Do you like your drama teacher?

2. Oui, _________ mon prof de _________ parce qu'il est _________.
   Yes, I love my drama teacher because he is funny.

3. Tu ________ ta prof d'espagnol?
   Do you like your Spanish teacher?

4. Non, je __________ _____ ma prof d'espagnol ________ ____'elle n'est pas _________.
   No, I don't like my Spanish teacher because she is not kind.

5. J'________ mon prof de sciences parce qu'____ _______ _________ en colère.
   I love my science teacher because he is never angry.

	Time 1	Time 2	Time 3	Time 4
Time				
Mistakes				

ASSESSMENT ROUND

1. Choose the correct translation (you won't need two of the sentences)

a. J'adore mon prof d'histoire parce qu'il est intelligent. _____

b. J'aime ma prof d'espagnol parce qu'elle est sympa. _____

c. Je n'aime pas mon prof de dessin parce qu'il est méchant. _____

d. Il aime son prof de sciences parce qu'il n'est pas impatient. _____

e. Elle adore sa prof d'informatique parce qu'elle est gentille. _____

1. I don't like my art teacher because he is mean.
2. She loves her IT teacher because she is kind.
3. I like my history teacher because he is intelligent.
4. I like my Spanish teacher because she is nice.
5. He likes his science teacher because he is not impatient.
6. She likes her IT teacher because she is kind.
7. I love my history teacher because he is intelligent.

2. Fill in the gaps with the missing words

a. Je m'appelle Isabelle et j'ai __________ ans.

b. J'__________ ma prof de français.

c. Elle est plus _______________ que ma prof d'allemand.

d. Je n'aime pas mon prof d'histoire parce qu'il est ____________.

e. Il est ________ sympathique que mon prof de géographie.

patiente	quinze	méchant	adore	moins

3. Translate the sentences into French

a. We like our IT teacher because he is interesting.

b. I don't like my technology teacher because she is not nice.

c. You (guys) love your music teacher because she is hard-working.

d. You don't like your science teacher because he is never in a good mood.

e. They like their English teacher because she is funny.

Main grammar focus:

- To conjugate *jouer*, *faire* and *aller* in the present indicative

Pop-up grammar:

- To use *au, à la, aux*
- To use *du, de la, de l'*

UNIT 11
Saying what I and others do in our free time

Que fais-tu pendant ton temps libre?	*What do you do in your free time?*
Que fait ton ami(e) pendant son temps libre?	*What does your friend do in his/her free time?*
Quels sports fais-tu?	*What sports do you do?*
Fais-tu d'autres activités?	*Do you do any other activities?*
Combien de fois par semaine fais-tu du sport?	*How many times a week do you do sport?*

Je joue	*I play*	**au basket** *basketball*		
Tu joues	*You play*	**au foot** *football*		
Il/Elle joue	*He/She plays*	**au tennis** *tennis*	**de temps en temps**	
Nous jouons	*We play*	**aux cartes** *cards*	*from time to time*	
Vous jouez	*You (guys) play*	**aux échecs** *chess*		
Ils/Elles jouent	*They play*	**avec des ami(e)s** *with some friends*	**deux fois par semaine**	
			twice a week	
		du footing *jogging*		
		du ski *skiing*	**pendant le week-end**	
Je fais	*I do*	**du sport** *sport*	*during the weekend*	
Tu fais	*You do*	**du vélo** *cycling*		
Il/Elle fait	*He/She does*	**de l'équitation** *horse riding*	**tous les jours**	
Nous faisons	*We do*	**de l'escalade** *rock climbing*	*every day*	
Vous faites	*You (guys) do*	**de la natation** *swimming*		
Ils/Elles font	*They do*	**de la randonnée** *hiking*	**tous les samedis**	
			every Saturday	
		au centre commercial *to the mall*		
		au centre sportif *to the sports centre*	**tous les soirs**	
		au gymnase *to the gym*	*every evening*	
Je vais	*I go*	**au parc** *to the park*		
Tu vas	*You go*	**à la campagne** *to the countryside*	**tous les week-ends**	
Il/Elle va	*He/She goes*	**à la montagne** *to the mountain*	*every weekend*	
Nous allons	*We go*	**à la pêche** *fishing*		
Vous allez	*You (guys) go*	**à la piscine** *to the pool*	**une fois par mois**	
Ils/Elles vont	*They go*	**à la plage** *to the beach*	*once a month*	
		chez des amis *to my friends' house*		
		en boîte *clubbing*		

MAIN GRAMMAR FOCUS
JOUER, FAIRE & ALLER

Jouer	Faire	Aller
To play	To do	To go
Je joue	**Je fais**	**Je vais**
I play	I do	I go
Tu joues	**Tu fais**	**Tu vas**
You play	You do	You go
Il/Elle joue	**Il/Elle fait**	**Il/Elle va**
He/She plays	He/She does	He/She goes
Nous jouons	**Nous faisons**	**Nous allons**
We play	We do	We go
Vous jouez	**Vous faites**	**Vous allez**
You (guys) play	You (guys) do	You (guys) go
Ils/Elles jouent	**Ils/Elles font**	**Ils/Elles vont**
They play	They do	They go

1. Match up

Je fais	He goes
Tu joues	We do
Il va	You (guys) go
Nous faisons	I do
Elles jouent	You (guys) do
Vous allez	They play
Vous faites	You play

2. Complete with the missing letters

a. J _ j _ _ e au basket.   *I play basketball.*

b. E _ _ e f _ _ t du vélo.   *She does cycling.*

c. V _ _ s all _ _ au parc.   *You (guys) go to the park.*

d. I _ _ v _ _ t à la plage.   *They go to the beach.*

e. N _ _ s f _ _ sons du ski.   *We do skiing.*

f. _ u _ ou _ _ aux cartes.   *You play cards.*

g. _ _ v _ _ _ _ à la plage.   *I go to the beach.*

3. Complete with the correct form of jouer, faire or aller

a. Je ___________ aux échecs.   *I play chess.*

b. Tu ___________ de l'équitation.   *You do horse riding.*

c. Ils ___________ au centre commercial.   *They go to the mall.*

d. Nous ___________ au tennis.   *We play tennis.*

e. Vous ___________ de la natation.   *You (guys) do swimming.*

f. Elles ___________ au centre sportif.   *They go to the sports centre.*

4. Break the flow

a. Tujouesauxcartestouslesjours.

b. Ilsfontdelanatationtouslessoirs.

c. Ilvaàlamontagneunefoisparmois.

d. Vousjouezauxéchecs?

e. Ellefaitdufootingdetempsentemps.

f. Jevaisaugymnasetouslesweekends.

g. Nousallonsàlapiscinetouslessoirs.

h. Iljoueavecdesamistouslessamedis.

5. Faulty translation: fix the English

a. Je vais à la campagne tous les soirs.
   I go to the countryside every Saturday.

b. Mon ami fait du vélo de temps en temps.
   My brother does cycling from time to time.

c. Tu joues au foot tous les jours.
   He plays football every day.

d. Nous faisons de l'escalade pendant le week-end.
   I go rock climbing during the weekend.

e. Elles vont à la piscine tous les week-ends.
   They go to the beach every weekend.

6. Choose the correct verb

a. Je **joue** / **joues** au tennis de temps en temps.

b. Nous **faisons** / **faites** du sport tous les soirs.

c. Vous **fais** / **faites** de la randonnée?

d. Tu **vais** / **vas** au parc tous les week-ends.

e. Elle **joues** / **joue** aux cartes tous les samedis.

f. Ils **vont** / **va** au gymnase deux fois par semaine.

g. Je **fais** / **fait** du footing pendant le week-end.

h. Tu **joue** / **joues** au foot une fois par mois.

7. Translate into French

a. I play chess from time to time.

b. She goes to the mall every day.

c. He does cycling every evening.

d. You go to the pool twice a week.

e. We do sport every weekend.

f. They (f) play basketball every day.

g. They (m) go to the park every Saturday.

h. You (guys) go to the gym twice a week.

8. Complete with the correct form of au, à la, aux, du, de la, de l'

a. Je joue _______________ tennis.　　*I play tennis.*

b. Vous faites _______________ sport.　　*You (guys) do sport.*

c. Elles vont _______________ piscine.　　*They go to the pool.*

d. Tu joues _______________ cartes.　　*You play cards.*

e. Nous faisons _______________ escalade.　　*We do rock climbing.*

f. Il va _______________ centre commercial.　　*He goes to the mall.*

g. Je joue _______________ échecs.　　*I play chess.*

h. Je fais _______________ randonnée.　　*I do hiking.*

POP-UP GRAMMAR
AU, À LA, AUX
DU, DE LA, DE L'

Jouer à is followed by a sport or a game.

- à followed by a masculine noun becomes **au**

  Je joue <u>au</u> football.   *I play football.*

- à followed by a feminine noun becomes **à la**

  Je joue <u>à la</u> pétanque.   *I play pétanque.*

- à followed by a plural noun becomes **aux**

  Je joue <u>aux</u> cartes.   *I play cards.*

Aller à is followed by a location or an activity that implies that you are going to a location.

- à followed by a masculine noun becomes **au**

  Je vais <u>au</u> parc.   *I go to the park.*

- à followed by a feminine noun becomes **à la**

  Je vais <u>à la</u> plage.   *I go to the beach.*

Faire de is followed by a sport or activity.

- de followed by a masculine noun becomes **du**

  Je fais <u>du</u> footing.   *I do jogging.*

- de followed by a feminine noun becomes **de la**

  Je fais <u>de la</u> natation.   *I do swimming.*

- de followed by a vowel or an H becomes **de l'**

  Je fais <u>de l'</u>équitation.   *I do horse riding.*

9. Match up

Je fais de l'équitation.	Do you play chess?
Il va à la montagne.	Do you do cycling?
Tu joues aux échecs?	You (guys) do swimming.
Vous faites de la natation.	I do horse riding.
Elles vont au centre sportif.	We play with some friends.
Tu fais du vélo?	They go to the sports centre.
Nous jouons avec des amis.	He goes to the mountain.

10. Slalom translation

Je vais	Tu fais	Il joue	Nous allons	Vous jouez	Elles font
aux	au	à la	de l'	du	au
ski	gymnase	basket	cartes	montagne	escalade
de temps	tous les	tous les	deux fois	pendant	une fois
par semaine	le week-end	en temps	par mois	soirs	week-ends

a. I go to the mountain once a month.

b. You do skiing every weekend.

c. He plays cards every evening.

d. We go to the gym during the weekend.

e. You (guys) play basketball twice a week.

f. They do rock climbing from time to time.

11. Translate into English

a. Je joue au tennis de temps en temps.

b. Nous faisons de la natation tous les jours.

c. Ils vont à la montagne une fois par mois.

d. Je fais de l'équitation tous les samedis.

e. Elles jouent aux échecs tous les soirs.

f. Vous allez à la pêche pendant le week-end.

g. Il fait du ski deux fois par semaine.

h. Tu vas au gymnase une fois par mois.

12. Spot and correct the errors

a. Je joue du basket tous les jours.

b. Ils font de natation tous les week-ends.

c. Il fait au tennis tous les soirs.

d. Tu vas à le gymnase une fois par jour.

e. Nous faisons de la escalade une fois par mois.

f. Vous allez à le parc tous les samedis.

g. Je fais sport pendant le week-end.

h. Elles jouent du ski de temps en temps.

13. Choose the correct answer

a. Je vais au **gymnase / parc / centre sportif**.   *I go to the sports centre.*

b. Vous faites du **sport / vélo / ski**.   *You (guys) do cycling.*

c. Nous jouons au **basket / tennis / foot**.   *We play basketball.*

d. Il fait de la **randonnée / natation / marche**.   *He does swimming.*

e. Tu vas à la **pêche / plage / piscine**.   *You go fishing.*

f. Elles jouent au **foot / basket / tennis**.   *They (f) play football.*

14. Arrange the words in the correct order.

a. aux échecs Je joue de temps en temps   *I play chess from time to time.*

b. Ils font deux fois de la randonnée par semaine   *They do hiking twice a week.*

c. pendant le week-end à la plage Elle va   *She goes to the beach during the weekend.*

d. aux cartes tous les jours Ils jouent   *They play cards every day.*

e. tous les samedis Elle fait de l'escalade   *She does rock climbing every Saturday.*

f. tous les soirs au gymnase Tu vas   *You go to the gym every evening.*

g. au foot Nous jouons tous les week-ends   *We play football every weekend.*

h. Vous faites une fois par mois du ski   *You (guys) do skiing once a month.*

15. Tangled translation

a. **I go** à la campagne **every weekend.**

b. Il fait **rock climbing** une fois **a month.**

c. Tu joues **cards from time to time.**

d. Elle va **to the mall** tous les jours.

e. **You (guys) do swimming** tous les samedis.

f. **They (m) play chess** pendant le week-end.

g. **We play tennis** deux fois par semaine.

h. **You go to the gym** de temps en temps.

16. Translate into French

a. I go to the mall every weekend.

b. He plays tennis twice a week.

c. You (guys) do horse riding every Saturday.

d. They (f) play football during the weekend.

e. You go to the countryside every day.

f. She plays chess every evening.

g. We do cycling from time to time.

h. They (m) go to the pool once a month.

UNIT 11 – ORAL PING PONG – Person A

ENGLISH	FRENCH	ENGLISH	FRENCH
I play basketball from time to time.	Je joue au basket de temps en temps.	He goes to the mountain during the weekend.	Il va à la montagne pendant le week-end.
He does jogging twice a week.		She plays chess every day.	
We go to the shopping mall during the weekend.	Nous allons au centre commercial pendant le week-end.	I go to the pool every Saturday.	Je vais à la piscine tous les samedis.
You do skiing once a month.		We do swimming every evening.	
He goes to the sports centre every day.	Il va au centre sportif tous les jours.	They (f) go to the beach every weekend.	Elles vont à la plage tous les week-ends.
She plays football every Saturday.		I play with some friends every day.	
I do cycling every evening.	Je fais du vélo tous les soirs.	He does hiking twice a week.	Il fait de la randonnée deux fois par semaine.
You (guys) go to the countryside every weekend.		You (guys) do rock climbing every Saturday.	
She plays cards from time to time.	Elle joue aux cartes de temps en temps.	I go to the beach once a month.	Je vais à la plage une fois par mois.
They (m) do horse riding twice a week.		They (m) go to the park every evening.	

UNIT 11 – ORAL PING PONG – Person B

ENGLISH	FRENCH	ENGLISH	FRENCH
I play basketball from time to time.		He goes to the mountain during the weekend.	
He does jogging twice a week.	Il fait du footing deux fois par semaine.	She plays chess every day.	Elle joue aux échecs tous les jours.
We go to the shopping mall during the weekend.		I go to the pool every Saturday.	
You do skiing once a month.	Tu fais du ski une fois par mois.	We do swimming every evening.	Nous faisons de la natation tous les soirs.
He goes to the sports centre every day.		They (f) go to the beach every weekend.	
She plays football every Saturday.	Elle joue au foot tous les samedis.	I play with some friends every day.	Je joue avec des amis tous les jours.
I do cycling every evening.		He does hiking twice a week.	
You (guys) go to the countryside every weekend.	Vous allez à la campagne tous les weekends.	You (guys) do rock climbing every Saturday.	Vous faites de l'escalade tous les samedis.
She plays cards from time to time.		I go to the beach once a month.	
They (m) do horse riding twice a week.	Ils font de l'équitation deux fois par semaine.	They (m) go to the park every evening.	Ils vont au parc tous les soirs.

No Snakes No Ladders 

DÉPART	**1** Je joue au basket.	**2** Tu vas au gymnase.	**3** Je fais du vélo.	**4** Elle va à la plage.	**5** de temps en temps	**6** Nous faisons de la randonnée.	**7** deux fois par semaine
15 Je vais à la campagne.	**14** Elle fait de la natation.	**13** Elles font de l'équitation.	**12** Il va à la montagne.	**11** Vous jouez au tennis.	**10** tous les jours	**9** Je fais du footing.	**8** Je vais à la pêche.
16 Je vais au centre sportif.	**17** tous les soirs	**18** Nous jouons au football.	**19** Elles jouent au basket.	**20** Je fais de la natation.	**21** Il va au centre commercial.	**22** Vous allez à la montagne.	**23** Je joue aux échecs.
ARRIVÉE	**30** Je fais du sport.	**29** Ils vont au parc.	**28** Je fais de l'escalade.	**27** Vous faites de la randonnée.	**26** Je joue aux cartes.	**25** Je fais du ski.	**24** Nous allons à la piscine.

No Snakes No Ladders

START	1	2	3	4	5	6	7
	I play basketball.	You go to the gym.	I do cycling.	She goes to the beach.	from time to time	We go hiking.	Twice a week
15	14	13	12	11	10	9	8
I go to the countryside.	She does swimming.	They (f) do horse riding.	He goes to the mountain.	You (guys) play tennis.	Every day	I do jogging.	I go fishing.
16	17	18	19	20	21	22	23
I go to the sports centre.	Every evening	We play football.	They (f) play basketball.	I do swimming.	He goes to the mall.	You (guys) go to the mountain.	I play chess.
FINISH	30	29	28	27	26	25	24
	I do sport.	They (m) go to the park.	I do rock climbing.	You (guys) do hiking.	I play cards.	I do skiing.	We go to the pool.

UNIT 11 – FAST & FURIOUS – ROUND 1

1. Bonjour. Que fais-tu pendant ton _________ _________?
   Hello. What do you do in your free time?

2. Je joue _________ tennis, je _________ de la natation et je _________ au parc.
   I play tennis, I do swimming and I go to the park.

3. Tu fais du _____________?
   Do you do cycling?

4. Non, mais mon père fait du vélo _________ ____ _________.
   No, but my father does cycling every day.

5. Ma mère ____ ____ _______________ tous les soirs.
   My mother goes to the gym every evening.

	Time 1	Time 2	Time 3	Time 4
Time				
Mistakes				

UNIT 11 – FAST & FURIOUS – ROUND 2

1. Bonjour. Que fais-tu pendant ton _________ _________?
   Hello. What do you do in your free time?

2. Je joue _________ échecs, je _________ du sport et je _________ au centre commercial.
   I play chess, I do sport and I go to the mall.

3. Tu fais de la _____________?
   Do you do swimming?

4. Non, mais mon frère fait de la natation _________ ____ _________ _________.
   No, but my brother does swimming once a week.

5. Ma sœur ____ ____ ____ _______________ pendant le week-end.
   My sister goes to the countryside during the weekend.

	Time 1	Time 2	Time 3	Time 4
Time				
Mistakes				

ASSESSMENT ROUND

1. Choose the correct translation (you won't need two of the sentences)

a. Je vais au centre sportif tous les soirs. _______

b. Elle va à la plage tous les samedis. _______

c. Tu joues aux cartes une fois par semaine. _______

d. Il fait de la natation de temps en temps. _______

e. Je fais de l'équitation une fois par mois. _______

1. You play cards once a week.
2. I do swimming from time to time.
3. I go to the sports centre every evening.
4. I do horse riding once a month.
5. You play cards twice a week.
6. She goes to the beach every Saturday.
7. He does swimming from time to time.

2. Fill in the gaps with the missing words

a. Je joue aux _________ de temps en temps.

b. Je _________ de la natation deux fois par semaine.

c. Je vais à la _________ pendant le week-end.

d. Il _________ aux échecs tous les jours.

e. Elle fait de l'_______________ tous les samedis.

pêche	cartes	équitation	fais	joue

3. Translate the sentences into French

a. I go to the gym every weekend.

b. He plays football twice a week.

c. You (guys) do cycling every Saturday.

d. We play tennis during the weekend.

e. They (m) go to the mountain every day.

Main grammar focus:

- To use reflexive verbs
(*se lever, s'habiller*…)
in the present indicative

Pop-up grammar:

- To conjugate irregular verbs
(*aller, faire, prendre, sortir*)

UNIT 12
Talking about my daily routine

Parle-moi de ta routine journalière.		*Tell me about your daily routine.*	
À quelle heure tu te lèves?		*What time do you get up?*	
Comment vas-tu au collège?		*How do you go to school?*	
Que fais-tu après le collège?		*What do you do after school?*	

		je me brosse les dents *I brush my teeth*	
		je me coiffe *I do my hair*	
		je me couche *I go to bed*	
Vers... *Around...*		**je déjeune** *I have lunch*	
À... *At*		**je dîne** *I have dinner*	
cinq heures *5*			
six heures *6*	**du matin**	**je fais mes devoirs** *I do my homework*	
sept heures *7*	*in the morning*		
huit heures cinq *8.05*		**je m'habille** *I get dressed*	
huit heures dix *8.10*		**je joue sur l'ordinateur** *I play on the computer*	**ensuite...** *then*
huit heures et quart *8.15*		**je me lève** *I get up*	
huit heures vingt *8.20*	**de l'après-midi**	**je me maquille**	**après...** *after*
huit heures vingt-cinq *8.25*	*in the afternoon*	*I put my make up on*	
huit heures et demie *8.30*		**je prends le petit-déjeuner**	
neuf heures moins vingt-cinq *8.35*			**finalement...** *finally*
neuf heures moins vingt *8.40*		*I have breakfast*	
neuf heures moins le quart *8.45*	**du soir**	**je regarde la télé** *I watch TV*	
neuf heures moins dix *8.50*	*in the evening*		
neuf heures moins cinq *8.55*		**je rentre à la maison** *I go back home*	
À midi *12pm*		**je me repose** *I rest*	
À minuit *12am*		**je sors de chez moi** *I leave my house*	
		je vais au collège en bus *I go to school by bus*	

MAIN GRAMMAR FOCUS
REFLEXIVE VERBS

A reflexive verb is when the subject acts on itself. For example:

se laver (*to wash oneself*) **se brosser les dents** (*to brush one's teeth*)
se coiffer (*to do one's hair*) **se coucher** (*to go to bed*)
s'habiller (*to get dressed*) **se lever** (*to get up*)

This is how they are conjugated:

Se lever	To get up	S'habiller	To get dressed
Je me lève	I get up	**Je m'habille**	I get dressed
Tu te lèves	You get up	**Tu t'habilles**	You get dressed
Il se lève	He gets up	**Il s'habille**	He gets dressed
Elle se lève	She gets up	**Elle s'habille**	She gets dressed

1. Match up

Je me lève	You shower
Il se couche	You have a wash
Tu te douches	She does her hair
Elle se coiffe	I get up
Je m'habille	He gets up
Tu te laves	I get dressed
Il se lève	He goes to bed

2. Complete with the missing letters

a. J _ m _ c _ _ ff _ . *I do my hair.*

b. _ l s'h _ b _ ll _ . *He gets dressed.*

c. T _ t _ l _ v _ s. *You get up.*

d. I _ s _ br _ ss _ les dents. *He brushes his teeth.*

e. J _ m _ c _ _ ch _ . *I go to bed.*

f. _ u t _ r _ p _ s _ s. *You rest.*

3. Complete with the correct form of me, te or se

a. Je _________ couche. *I go to bed.*

b. Il _________ lève. *He gets up.*

c. Tu _________ brosses les dents. *You brush your teeth.*

d. Elle _________ coiffe. *She does her hair.*

e. Je _________ maquille. *I put my makeup on.*

f. Tu _________ habilles. *You get dressed.*

g. Elle _________ réveille. *She wakes up.*

h. Il _________ rase. *He shaves.*

4. Break the flow

a. Àhuitheuresjemerepose.

b. Àseptheuresjemebrosselesdents.

c. Àneufheurescinqjemelève.

d. Àminuittutecouches.

e. Àsixheuresetdemieilsebrosselesdents.

f. Àdixheuresdixellesecoiffe.

g. Àseptheuresetquartjemhabille.

h. Àdixheurestutelèves.

5. Faulty translation: fix the English

a. À neuf heures je me lève.
   At 9:00, I wake up.

b. À dix heures cinq je m'habille.
   At 9:05, I get dressed.

c. À dix heures et demie je me coiffe.
   At 10:30, I brush my teeth.

d. À cinq heures je me repose.
   At 5:00, I read.

e. À minuit je me couche.
   At 12:00, I have a shower.

6. Choose the correct verb

a. Je **m'habille / t'habilles** à sept heures et quart.

b. Mon frère **se coiffe / te coiffes** à neuf heures.

c. Tu **se repose / te reposes** à quatre heures?

d. Je **te lèves / me lève** à six heures et demie.

e. Elle **se brosse / me brosse** les dents.

f. Il **te couche / se couche** à onze heures.

g. Je **me coiffe / se coiffe** à huit heures dix.

h. Tu **te lèves / me lève** à six heures vingt.

7. Translate into French

a. I get up at 6:00.

b. I brush my teeth at 6:15.

c. I get dressed at 6:30.

d. I do my hair at 6:45.

e. I rest at 5:00.

f. I go to bed at 11:00.

g. My father gets up at 8:15.

h. He rests at 8:00.

8. Complete with the correct form of aller, faire, prendre or sortir

a. Je _________________ mes devoirs. *I do my homework.*

b. Je _________________ de chez moi. *I leave my house.*

c. Je _________________ au collège en bus. *I go to school by bus.*

d. Je _________________ le petit-déjeuner. *I have breakfast.*

e. Il _________________ au collège en bus. *He goes to school by bus.*

f. Tu _________________ tes devoirs. *You do your homework.*

g. Elle _________________ de chez elle. *She leaves her house.*

h. Il _________________ le petit-déjeuner. *He has breakfast.*

POP-UP GRAMMAR
IRREGULAR VERBS

Some verbs are called irregular verbs because they have a pattern of their own. The ones in this unit are **aller**, **faire**, **prendre** and **sortir**.

This is how they are conjugated:

Aller	*To go*	Faire	*To do*	Prendre	*To take*	Sortir	*To leave*
Je vais	*I go*	**Je fais**	*I do*	**Je prends**	*I take*	**Je sors**	*I leave*
Tu vas	*You go*	**Tu fais**	*You do*	**Tu prends**	*You take*	**Tu sors**	*You leave*
Il va	*He goes*	**Il fait**	*He does*	**Il prend**	*He takes*	**Il sort**	*He leaves*
Elle va	*She goes*	**Elle fait**	*She does*	**Elle prend**	*She takes*	**Elle sort**	*She leaves*

9. Match up

Je prends le petit-déjeuner.	I go to school by bus.
Il sort de chez lui.	I have breakfast.
Je sors de chez moi.	She has breakfast.
Tu fais tes devoirs.	I leave my house.
Je fais mes devoirs.	He leaves his house.
Elle prend le petit-déjeuner.	You do your homework.
Je vais au collège en bus.	I do my homework.

10. Slalom translation

À six heures	Ensuite je	À huit heures	Il rentre	Tu te brosses	Tu fais
il dîne	et quart	à la	regarde	tes devoirs	les dents
et	et il	je me	et tu joues	maison	la télé
après	et je sors	et il	lève et	se	sur
de chez moi	l'ordinateur	repose	tu t'habilles	je me coiffe	se couche

a. At 6:15, I get up and I do my hair.

b. Then, I watch TV and I leave my house.

c. At 8:00, he has dinner and he rests.

d. He goes back home and goes to bed.

e. You brush your teeth and after you get dressed.

f. You do your homework and you play on the computer.

11. Translate into English

a. À huit heures je me réveille.

b. Ensuite je me lève.

c. À huit heures et quart je me douche.

d. Après je m'habille et je me maquille.

e. Mon frère se lève à six heures et demie.

f. Ensuite il se lave et il se rase.

g. À dix heures du soir il se couche.

h. Et toi, tu te lèves à quelle heure?

12. Spot and correct the errors

a. Je te lève à huit heures cinq.

b. Ensuite je douche me.

c. Après je me habille dans ma chambre.

d. Je sor de chez moi.

e. Je vas au collège en bus.

f. Ma sœur prends le petit-déjeuner.

g. Elle vae au gymnase.

h. Tu me reposes de temps en temps.

13. Choose the correct answer

a. Je **me lave / me lève / me repose**.   *I rest.*

b. Tu **vas au collège / fais tes devoirs / sors de chez toi**.   *You do your homework.*

c. Il se **couche / réveille / coiffe**.   *He goes to bed.*

d. Elle **déjeune / dîne / fait ses devoirs**.   *She has lunch.*

e. Je **rentre à la maison / sors de chez moi**.   *I leave my house.*

f. Tu te **brosses les dents / coiffes / laves**.   *You do your hair.*

14. Arrange the words in the correct order.

a. À six heures je me réveille du matin   *At 6:00, I wake up.*

b. je À six heures et quart lève me   *At 6:15, I get up.*

c. je me douche À six heures et demie   *At 6:30, I shower.*

d. je prends À sept heures, le petit-déjeuner   *At 7:00, I have breakfast.*

e. les dents je me brosse À sept heures vingt   *At 7:20, I brush my teeth.*

f. moins le quart, je sors de chez moi À huit heures   *At 7:45, I leave my house.*

g. au collège tous les jours Je vais en bus   *I go to school by bus every day.*

h. À sept heures je me repose du soir   *At 7:00 in the evening, I rest.*

---

15. Guided translation: complete the translation

a. I get dressed and after I do my hair.   Je m'_________ et après je me _________ .

b. He watches TV at midday.   Il _________ la télé à _________ .

c. At what time do you get up?   À quelle heure tu ___ _________?

d. She goes back home and rests.   Elle _________ à la maison et se _________ .

e. I go to bed at midnight.   Je ___ _________ à minuit.

f. I get dressed and I leave my house.   Je ___'_________ et je _____ de chez moi.

---

16. Tangled translation

a. À sept heures et demie **I brush** les dents.

b. Ensuite **I leave** de chez moi.

c. Après **I go** au collège **by bus.**

d. À midi **she has lunch** à la cantine.

e. Elle **goes back** à la maison.

f. Je **watch** la télé et je **rest.**

g. À neuf heures je **do my homework.**

h. Je **go to bed** à onze heures et quart.

17. Translate into French

a. I get up at 6:00.

b. I have a wash and I get dressed.

c. Then I have my breakfast.

d. After I brush my teeth.

e. I leave the house at 7:30.

f. I go to school by bus.

g. My sister goes to school by car.

h. I go back home at 5:00.

No Snakes No Ladders

	1 Je vais.	2 Je me lève.	3 Je fais.	4 Il se couche.	5 Je sors.	6 Tu t'habilles.	7 Je prends.
DÉPART							
15 Il se lève.	14 Il prend.	13 Tu vas.	12 Je me repose.	11 Il sort.	10 Tu fais.	9 Elle se couche.	8 Elle se lève.
16 Elle sort.	17 Tu te couches.	18 Je me coiffe.	19 Il va.	20 Elle prend.	21 Elle se coiffe.	22 Elle fait.	23 Tu sors.
ARRIVÉE	30 Tu te lèves.	29 Il fait.	28 Tu prends.	27 Je me couche.	26 Elle va.	25 Il se repose.	24 Elle s'habille.

No Snakes No Ladders

START	**1** I go.	**2** I get up.	**3** I do.	**4** He goes to bed.	**5** I leave.	**6** You get dressed.	**7** I take.
15 He gets up.	**14** He takes.	**13** You go.	**12** I rest.	**11** He leaves.	**10** You do.	**9** She goes to bed.	**8** She gets up.
16 She leaves.	**17** You go to bed.	**18** I do my hair.	**19** He goes.	**20** She takes.	**21** She does her hair.	**22** She does.	**23** You leave.
FINISH	**30** You get up.	**29** He does.	**28** You take.	**27** I go to bed.	**26** She goes.	**25** He rests.	**24** She gets dressed.

UNIT 12 – FAST & FURIOUS – ROUND 1

1. Bonjour. À quelle heure tu _____ _______?
    Hello. At what time do you get up?

2. Je _____ _______ à sept heures et je _____ _______ à onze heures.
    I get up at seven and I go to bed at 11:00.

3. Comment ______-____ au collège?
    How do you go to school?

4. Je _____ au collège en _______.
    I go to school by bus.

5. Ma sœur s'__________ et ensuite elle se _______.
    My sister gets dressed and then she does her hair.

	Time 1	Time 2	Time 3	Time 4
Time				
Mistakes				

UNIT 12 – FAST & FURIOUS – ROUND 2

1. Bonjour. À quelle heure tu _____ _______?
    Hello. At what time do you go to bed?

2. Je _____ _______ à dix heures et je _____ _______ à cinq heures.
    I go to bed at 10:00 and I get up at 5:00.

3. Comment ______-____ au collège?
    How do you go to school?

4. Je _____ au collège en ____________.
    I go to school by car.

5. Mon frère se __________ et ensuite il _______ la télé.
    My brother rests and then he watches TV.

	Time 1	Time 2	Time 3	Time 4
Time				
Mistakes				

ASSESSMENT ROUND

1. Choose the correct translation (you won't need two of the sentences)

a. À sept heures et demie je me douche et après je m'habille. _____

b. À huit heures, je prends le petit-déjeuner. _____

c. À huit heures vingt, il se brosse les dents. _____

d. À huit heures moins le quart, elle va au collège. _____

e. Il joue sur l'ordinateur et il regarde la télé. _____

1. At 7:45, she goes to school.
2. At 7:30 I shower and then I get dressed.
3. He plays on the computer and he watches TV.
4. He rests and he watches TV.
5. At 8:20, he does his hair.
6. At 8:00, I have breakfast.
7. At 8:20, he brushes his teeth.

2. Fill in the gaps with the missing words

a. Je me ___________ toujours vers six heures et demie.

b. Ensuite, je me douche et je m'___________ après.

c. Je ___________ au collège en vélo vers sept heures et quart.

d. Je ___________ à la maison vers quatre heures et quart.

e. Ensuite je me ___________ un peu.

rentre	habille	repose	vais	réveille

3. Translate the sentences into French

a. I get up at 6:30.

b. I have my breakfast at 8:00.

c. I go back home and I watch TV.

d. I go to bed at midnight.

e. I have dinner at 8:45.

UNIT 13 – Talking about weekend plans

Main grammar focus:

- To form and use the immediate future

UNIT 13
Talking about weekend plans

Quels sont tes projets pour le week-end prochain?	*What are your plans for next weekend?*
Où voudrais-tu aller?	*Where would you like to go?*
Quels sont les projets de ton frère/ta sœur?	*What are your brother/sister's plans?*
Où va aller ton frère/ta sœur?	*Where is your brother/sister going to go?*

			centre commercial	*shopping mall*
Le week-end prochain *Next weekend*	**je vais aller** *I am going to go* **je voudrais aller** *I would like to go*	**au**	centre sportif	*sports centre*
			cinéma	*cinema*
			gymnase	*gym*
			parc	*park*
	ma sœur va aller *my sister is going to go*		stade	*stadium*
Vendredi *On Friday*	**mon ami(e) va aller** *my friend is going to go*	**à la**	pêche	*fishing*
			piscine	*pool*
Samedi *On Saturday*	**mon frère va aller** *my brother is going to go*		plage	*beach*
		en	boîte	*clubbing*
		faire	les magasins	*shopping*
	nous allons aller *we are going to go*	**me (je)** **se (il/elle)**	promener	*for a walk*

				acheter des choses	*buy things*
...avec *...with*	**ma (f)** **mon (m)** *my* **sa** **son** *his/her*	**frère** *brother* **meilleure amie** *best friend (f)* **meilleur ami** *best friend (m)* **petite amie** *girlfriend* **petit ami** *boyfriend* **sœur** *sister*	**pour** *(in order) to*	acheter des vêtements	*buy clothes*
				bronzer	*sunbathe*
				danser	*dance*
				faire de la musculation	*do bodybuilding*
				faire du vélo	*ride my bike*
				jouer au foot	*play football*
				nager	*swim*
				regarder un film	*watch a film*
				regarder/voir un match	*watch/see a match*

Ce sera amusant	Ce sera ennuyeux	Ce sera fatigant	Ce sera relaxant
It will be fun	*It will be boring*	*It will be tiring*	*It will be relaxing*

MAIN GRAMMAR FOCUS
THE IMMEDIATE FUTURE

The immediate future is used to express what you are going to do in the near future.

Example:

Je <u>vais</u> aller au parc cet après-midi
I <u>am going</u> to go to the park this afternoon

To form the immediate future, you need to use the verb **aller** in the present tense and the infinitive afterwards, just like in the grid below:

Je	*I*	**vais**	*am going*		
Tu	*You*	**vas**	*are going*	**aller**	*to go*
Il/Elle	*He/She*	**va**	*is going*	**acheter**	*to buy*
Nous	*We*	**allons**	*are going*	**faire**	*to do*
Vous	*You (guys)*	**allez**	*are going*	**jouer**	*to play*
Ils/Elles	*They*	**vont**	*are going*		

1. Match up

Je vais aller	He is going to dance
Tu vas faire	We are going to play
Il va danser	You (guys) are going to watch
Elle va nager	I am going to go
Nous allons jouer	She is going to swim
Vous allez regarder	They are going to buy
Ils vont acheter	You are going to do

2. Complete with the missing letters

a. J _ v _ _ s _ ll _ r au parc.
I am going to go to the park.

b. _ l v _ f _ _ r _ les magasins.
He is going to go shopping.

c. I _ _ v _ _ t _ ll _ r en boîte.
They (m) are going to go clubbing.

d. _ ll _ s v _ _ t se pr _ m _ n _ r.
They (f) are going to go for a walk.

e. T _ v _ s _ ronz _ r à la plage.
You are going to sunbathe at the beach.

3. Complete with the correct form of vais, vas or va

a. Je ___________ acheter des choses.   *I am going to buy things.*

b. Il ___________ acheter des vêtements.   *He is going to buy clothes.*

c. Tu ___________ te promener.   *You are going to go for a walk.*

d. Elle ___________ bronzer.   *She is going to sunbathe.*

e. Nous ___________ faire de la musculation.   *We are going to do bodybuilding.*

f. Vous ___________ faire du vélo.   *You (guys) are going to ride your bike.*

g. Elles ___________ regarder un film.   *They are going to watch a film.*

h. Ils ___________ aller en boîte.   *They are going to go clubbing.*

4. Break the flow

a. Vendredijevaisalleràlapiscine.

b. Leweekendprochainilsvontallerauparc.

c. Samediellevafairelesmagasins.

d. Leweekendprochaintuvasalleraustade.

e. Vendredivousallezzallerenboîte.

f. Leweekendprochainilvaallleraucinéma.

g. Samedinousallonsalleraucentresportif.

h. Vendredijevaisalleraucentrecommercial.

5. Faulty translation: fix the English

a. Je vais aller faire les magasins.
On Saturday, I am going to go shopping.

b. Samedi elle va aller au parc.
On Saturday, he is going to go to the park.

c. Vous allez aller à la plage.
We are going to go to the beach .

d. Tu vas aller en boîte.
You are going to go in a box.

e. Elles vont aller se promener.
They are going to go for a run.

6. Choose the correct verb

a. Je **vais / va** aller au centre commercial.

b. Mon frère **vas / va** aller au centre sportif.

c. Tu **vas / va** aller au cinéma.

d. Nous **allez / allons** aller à la pêche.

e. Elles **va / vont** aller à la piscine.

f. Elle **vais / va** aller en boîte.

g. Vous **allons / allez** vous promener.

h. Ils **vas / vont** aller au stade.

7. Translate into French

a. I am going to go to the gym.

b. She is going to go to the park.

c. You (guys) are going to go to the mall.

d. They (m) are going to go to the pool.

e. We are going to go clubbing.

f. He is going to go for a walk.

g. You are going to go fishing.

h. They (f) are going to go to the cinema.

8. Slalom translation

Vendredi	Samedi	Dimanche	Dimanche	Vendredi	Samedi
vous	je	elles	tu	il	nous
va aller	vais aller	vont aller	allez aller	vas faire	allons aller
à la	les	en	au	au	au
boîte	parc	stade	pêche	magasins	gymnase

a. On Friday, I am going to go to the gym.

b. On Saturday, you (guys) are going to go clubbing.

c. On Sunday, he is going to go fishing.

d. On Sunday, we are going to go to the park.

e. On Friday, you are going to go shopping.

f. On Saturday, they (f) are going to go to the stadium.

9. Translate into English

a. Vendredi je vais jouer au foot.

b. Le week-end prochain il va danser.

c. Samedi elles vont voir un match.

d. Dimanche tu vas aller à la pêche.

e. Nous allons aller au stade.

f. Sa petite amie va bronzer à la plage.

g. Mes frères vont nager à la piscine.

h. Samedi vous allez acheter des vêtements.

10. Spot and correct the errors

a. Je vais aller à le gymnase.

b. Ensuite je vais aller en pêche.

c. Après mon frère va danser à la boîte.

d. Mon ami va aller à le centre commercial.

e. Nous allons allé au parc.

f. Vous allez aller au piscine pour nager.

g. Elles aller va au gymnase.

h. Tu vas bronzer à le parc.

11. Choose the correct answer

a. Je vais aller au **centre sportif / stade / parc**.   *I'm going to go to the stadium.*

b. Tu vas aller **au cinéma / au gymnase / à la piscine**.   *You're going to go to the pool.*

c. Ils vont aller **à la pêche / en boîte / au gymnase**.   *They are going to go fishing.*

d. Elle va aller à la **plage / montagne / campagne**.   *She's going to go to the beach.*

e. Je vais aller **faire les magasins / faire du vélo / nager**.   *I'm going to go shopping.*

f. Vous allez aller **en boîte / en ville / en France**.   *You (guys) are going to go to town.*

12. Arrange the words in the correct order.

a. je vais aller avec ma sœur Samedi à la plage.
   On Saturday, I am going to go to the beach with my sister.

b. au stade tu vas aller avec ton meilleur ami Dimanche.
   On Sunday, you are going to go to the stadium with your best friend.

c. mon frère va aller Le week-end prochain pour danser en boîte.
   Next weekend, my brother is going to go clubbing to dance.

d. Samedi au parc vont aller mes amies pour bronzer.
   On Saturday, my friends are going to go to the park to sunbathe.

e. au gymnase Vendredi pour faire de la musculation vous allez aller.
   On Friday, you (guys) are going to go the gym to do bodybuilding.

f. des vêtements Le week-end prochain nous allons acheter.
   Next weekend, we are going to buy clothes.

---

13. Guided translation: complete the translation

a. *My brother is going to watch a film.*   Mon frère _____ _________ un film.

b. *My sisters are going to go to the park.*   Mes sœurs _____ aller _____ parc.

c. *On Friday, I am going to go to the gym.*   Vendredi je _____ aller _____ gymnase.

d. *You are going to go to the beach.*   Tu _____ aller ___ ___ plage.

e. *We are going to watch a match.*   Nous _______ _________ un match.

f. *You (guys) are going to go fishing.*   Vous _______ aller ___ ___ pêche.

---

14. Tangled translation

a. Vendredi **I am going** voir un match.

b. Samedi **you (guys) are going** nager.

c. Nous allons aller **to the shopping mall.**

d. Elle **is going to go to the** piscine.

e. Ils vont aller **to go for a walk.**

f. Ma sœur **is going to** faire du vélo.

g. **You are going** bronzer **at the beach.**

h. Ils vont **do bodybuilding at the** gymnase.

15. Translate into French

a. My sister is going to go shopping.

b. I am going to go to the gym.

c. You are going to sunbathe at the park.

d. We are going to buy things.

e. You (guys) are going to buy clothes.

f. He is going to do bodybuilding.

g. They (f) are going to swim.

h. I am going to ride my bike.

No Snakes No Ladders

DÉPART

1	Je vais aller au cinéma.
2	Tu vas aller au centre sportif.
3	Il va bronzer à la plage.
4	Elle va danser en boîte.
5	Nous allons faire de la musculation.
6	Vous allez faire du vélo au parc.
7	Ils vont jouer au foot au stade.
8	Tu vas aller à la pêche.
9	Elles vont voir un match.
10	Il va nager à la piscine.
11	Elle va regarder un film.
12	Je vais aller au centre commercial.
13	Vous allez aller au cinéma.
14	Tu vas aller au centre commercial.
15	Je vais acheter des choses.
16	Qu'est-ce que tu vas faire vendredi?
17	Nous allons aller à la piscine avec ma sœur.
18	Il va aller au parc pour faire du vélo.
19	Où vas-tu aller vendredi?
20	Elles vont aller à la piscine.
21	Nous allons aller à la plage avec nos amis.
22	Tu vas aller en boîte.
23	Elle va aller se promener.
24	Je vais regarder un film.
25	Qu'est-ce que tu vas faire le week-end prochain?
26	Je vais aller me promener.
27	Je vais aller à la pêche avec mon petit ami.
28	Vous allez acheter des vêtements.
29	Ils vont aller au centre commercial pour acheter des choses.
30	Je vais aller en boîte.

ARRIVÉE

No Snakes No Ladders

START

1. I am going to go to the cinema.
2. You are going to go to the sports centre.
3. He is going to sunbathe at the beach.
4. She is going to go clubbing.
5. We are going to do bodybuilding.
6. You (guys) are going to ride a bike at the park.
7. They (m) are going to play football at the stadium.
8. You are going to go fishing.
9. They (f) are going to see a match.
10. He is going to swim at the pool.
11. She is going to watch a film.
12. I am going to go to the shopping mall.
13. You (guys) are going to go to the cinema.
14. You are going to go to the shopping mall.
15. I am going to buy things.
16. What are you going to do on Friday?
17. We are going to go to the pool with my sister.
18. He is going to go to the park to ride his bike.
19. Where are you going to go on Friday?
20. They (f) are going to go to the pool.
21. We are going to go to the beach with our friends.
22. You are going to go clubbing.
23. She is going to go for a walk.
24. I am going to watch a film.
25. What are you going to do next weekend?
26. I am going to go for a walk.
27. I am going to go fishing with my boyfriend.
28. You (guys) are going to buy clothes.
29. They (m) are going to go to the shopping mall to buy things.
30. I am going to go clubbing.

FINISH

THE LANGUAGE GYM
GRAMMAR BOOKLET I

UNIT 13 – FAST & FURIOUS – ROUND 1

1. Bonjour. Qu'est-ce que tu ____ ________ le week-end prochain?
   Hello. What are you going to do next weekend?

2. Je ____ ________ au centre commercial pour ________ ____ ________.
   I am going to go to the shopping mall to buy things.

3. Où ___ _____ ton frère?
   Where is your brother going to go?

4. Il ____ aller ____ gymnase pour faire de la ____________.
   He is going to go to the gym to do bodybuilding.

5. Ma meilleure amie ____ aller ___ ___ plage pour __________.
   My best friend is going to go to the beach to sunbathe.

	Time 1	Time 2	Time 3	Time 4
Time				
Mistakes				

UNIT 13 – FAST & FURIOUS – ROUND 2

1. Bonjour. Qu'est-ce que tu ____ ________ le week-end prochain?
   Hello. What are you going to do next weekend?

2. Je ____ ________ au stade pour ______ ____ ________.
   I am going to go to the stadium to see a match.

3. Où ___ _____ ta sœur?
   Where is your sister going to go?

4. Elle ____ aller ____ parc pour faire du ________.
   She is going to go to the park to ride her bike.

5. Mon meilleur ami ____ aller ___ ___ piscine pour __________.
   My best friend is going to go to the pool to swim.

	Time 1	Time 2	Time 3	Time 4
Time				
Mistakes				

ASSESSMENT ROUND

1. Choose the correct translation (you won't need two of the sentences)

a. Le week-end prochain je vais aller au cinéma avec mon petit ami. _____

b. Samedi, je vais aller faire les magasins avec ma sœur. _____

c. Vendredi, je vais aller au stade avec mes amis pour voir un match. _____

d. Le week-end prochain je vais aller me promener avec mon ami. _____

e. Qu'est-ce que tu vas faire le week-end prochain? _____

1. Where are you going to go next weekend?
2. On Friday, I am going to go to the stadium with my friends to see a match.
3. Next weekend, I am going to go to the cinema with my girlfriend.
4. Next weekend, I am going to go for a walk with my friend.
5. What are you going to do next weekend?
6. On Saturday, I am going to go shopping with my sister.
7. Next weekend, I am going to go to the cinema with my boyfriend.

2. Fill in the gaps with the missing words

a. Vendredi, je vais voir un film _____ cinéma.

b. Samedi, tu _____ nager à la piscine.

c. Je _____ aller au centre commercial pour acheter des vêtements.

d. Elle va aller _____ piscine avec sa sœur pour nager.

e. Je vais _____ me promener au parc avec mon frère.

vais	au	aller	vas	à la

3. Translate the sentences into French

a. I am going to go to the shopping mall with my friends.

b. You (guys) are going to go for a walk at the park.

c. She is going to go fishing with her friends (f) at the beach.

d. What are you going to do on Friday?

e. We are going to swim at the pool.

UNIT 14
Talking about food:
likes, dislikes, reasons

Main grammar focus:

- To review conjugation of verbs like aimer. Review of verb être.
- To review adjectival agreements (masc/fem/plural).

Pop-up grammar:

- To conjugate *préférer*

Unit 14. Talking about food: likes, dislikes, reasons

Qu'est-ce que tu aimes manger et boire? Pourquoi? *What do you like to eat and drink? Why?*			
J'adore *I love* **J'aime beaucoup** *I like a lot*	**le café** *coffee* **le chocolat** *chocolate* **le fromage** *cheese* **le jus de fruits** *fruit juice* **le lait** *milk* **le miel** *honey* **le pain** *bread* **le poisson** *fish* **le poulet rôti** *roast chicken* **le riz** *rice* **la salade verte** *green salad* **la viande** *meat* **l'eau** *water* (l' + vowel)	***parce que c'est** *because it is*	**dégoûtant** *disgusting* **délicieux** *delicious* **dur** *hard* **épicé** *spicy* **gras** *greasy* **juteux** *juicy* **malsain** *unhealthy* **rafraîchissant** *refreshing* **sain** *healthy* **savoureux** *tasty* **sucré** *sweet*
J'aime *I like* **J'aime un peu** *I like a bit* **Je n'aime pas** *I don't like*	**les chocolats** *chocolates* **les fruits** *fruit* **les hamburgers** *burgers* **les légumes** *vegetables* **les œufs** *eggs*	****parce qu'ils sont** *because they are*	**dégoûtants** *disgusting* **délicieux** *delicious* **durs** *hard* **épicés** *spicy* **gras** *greasy* **juteux** *juicy* **malsains** *unhealthy* **rafraîchissants** *refreshing* **sains** *healthy* **savoureux** *tasty* **sucrés** *sweet*
Je déteste *I hate* **Je préfère** *I prefer*	**les bananes** *bananas* **les fraises** *strawberries* **les crevettes** *prawns* **les oranges** *oranges* **les pommes** *apples* **les tomates** *tomatoes*	**parce qu'elles sont** *because they are*	**dégoûtantes** *disgusting* **délicieuses** *delicious* **dures** *hard* **épicées** *spicy* **grasses** *greasy* **juteuses** *juicy* **malsaines** *unhealthy* **rafraîchissantes** *refreshing* **saines** *healthy* **savoureuses** *tasty* **sucrées** *sweet*

PLEASE NOTE

* After "c'est" an adjective is always in its masculine singular form

E.g. J'aime la viande, c'est délicieux.

** However, in the second section after "ils sont" or "elles sont", adjectives agree both in gender and number

E.g. J'aime les œufs parce qu'ils sont sains / J'aime les tomates parce qu'elles sont saines.

MAIN GRAMMAR FOCUS
ADJECTIVES

An adjective is used to describe a noun.

After *c'est,* an adjective is always in its masculine singular form.

> J'aime la viande, **c'est délicieux.**
> *I like meat, **it's delicious**.*

However, after *ils sont* or *elles sont*, adjectives agree both in **gender** and **number**.

> J'aime les œufs parce qu'**ils sont sains**.
> *I like eggs because **they are healthy**.*

> J'aime les tomates parce qu'**elles sont saines**.
> *I like tomatoes because **they are healthy**.*

If the adjective ends with a **consonant** or *-é*, you add an *-s* in the masculine plural form and *-es* in the feminine plural form

> Ils sont dégoûtant**s**.   Elles sont dégoûtant**es**.
> *They are disgusting **(m)**.*   *They are digusting **(f)**.*

> **Ils sont sucrés**.   **Elles sont sucrées**.
> *They are sweet **(m)**.*   *They are sweet **(f)**.*

If the adjective ends with *-eux*, you don't add anything in the masculine plural form and you will change *-eux* into *-euses* in the feminine plural form

> **Ils sont délicieux**.   **Elles sont délicieuses**.
> *They are delicious **(m)**.*   *They are delicious **(f)**.*

If the adjective ends with *-s*, you don't add anything in the masculine plural form and you add *-ses* in the feminine plural form

> **Ils sont gras**.   **Elles sont grasses**.
> *They are greasy **(m)**.*   *They are greasy **(f)**.*

1. Match up

c'est délicieux	it is spicy
c'est épicé	they are juicy
ils sont sains	it is delicious
elles sont sucrées	they are hard
ils sont juteux	they are healthy
elles sont dures	it is unhealthy
c'est malsain	they are sweet

2. Complete with the missing letters

a. _ ls s _ nt d _ l _ c _ _ _ x.
   They are delicious.

b. C' _ st s _ v _ _ r _ _ x.
   It is tasty.

c. _ ll _ s s _ nt r _ fr _ _ ch _ ss _ nt _ s.
   They are refreshing.

d. C' _ st d _ g _ _ t _ nt.
   It is disgusting.

3. Complete with the missing words

a. J'adore le miel parce que _______ sucré.   *I like honey because it is sweet.*

b. Ils aiment les fruits parce qu'___ ______ sains.   *They like fruit because they are healthy.*

c. Tu préfères le poisson parce que c'est ________ .   *You prefer fish because it is delicious.*

d. Elle aime les oranges. Elles sont ______ .   *She likes oranges. They are juicy.*

e. Nous n'aimons pas le riz parce que ______ dur.   *We don't like rice because it is hard.*

f. Tu aimes les œufs parce qu'___ ______ savoureux.   *You like eggs because they are tasty.*

g. Vous aimez les légumes. Ils sont ______________ .   *You (guys) like vegs. They are refreshing.*

h. Il préfère ___ ______ ______ parce que c'est ______ .   *He prefers green salad because it is healthy.*

4. Break the flow

a. Vousaimezlemielparcequecestsucré.

b. Jenaimepaslaviandeparcequecestgras.

c. Ilaimelesbananesparcequellessontsaines.

d. Jedétestelesœufsparcequilssontmalsains.

e. Nousaimonslasaladeverteparcequecestsain.

f. Jaimelesfraisesparcequellessontsucrées.

g. Jepréfèrelerizparcequecestsavoureux.

h. Ilsadorentleauparcequecestrafraîchissant.

5. Faulty translation: fix the English

a. J'aime le chocolat parce que c'est sucré.
   I like chocolate because it is delicious.

b. Ils détestent les fraises. Elles sont dures.
   I don't like strawberries. They are hard.

c. Nous aimons le fromage. C'est délicieux.
   You (guys) like cheese. It is tasty.

d. Je n'aime pas le riz parce que c'est dur.
   I don't like rice because it is unhealthy.

e. J'aime les oranges. Elles sont juteuses.
   I like oranges. They are refreshing.

6. Choose the correct verb	**7. Translate into French**

6. Choose the correct verb

a. Vous aimez la viande. **C'est / Elles sont** savoureux.

b. Je déteste les hamburgers. **Ils sont / Il est** gras.

c. Nous n'aimons pas le miel. **C'est / Ils sont** sucré.

d. Je préfère les légumes. **C'est / Ils sont** sains.

e. Ils aiment les tomates. **C'est / Elles sont** juteuses.

f. Je préfère le lait. **C'est / Ils sont** délicieux.

g. Elle déteste le poisson. **C'est / Ils sont** dégoûtant.

h. Je préfère le poulet rôti. **C'est / Ils sont** épicé.

7. Translate into French

a. It is refreshing.

b. They (m) are juicy.

c. It is healthy.

d. They (f) are sweet.

e. It is delicious.

f. They (m) are hard.

g. It is unhealthy.

h. They (f) are disgusting.

8. Complete with the missing verbs

a. Je ________ le chocolat parce que c'est sucré. — *I prefer chocolate because it is sweet.*

b. Il ________ les pommes parce qu'elles sont dures. — *He likes apples because they are hard.*

c. Je ________ le pain parce que c'est délicieux. — *I prefer bread because it is delicious.*

d. Nous ________ les oranges. Elles sont saines. — *We like oranges. They are healthy.*

e. Je ________ ____ le lait parce que c'est dégoûtant. — *I don't like milk because it is disgusting.*

f. Tu ______ les crevettes. Elles sont savoureuses. — *You like prawns. They are tasty.*

g. Elles ________ les légumes. Ils sont sains. — *They love vegetables. They are healthy.*

h. Je ________ les fruits. Ils sont rafraîchissants. — *I prefer fruit. They are refreshing.*

POP-UP GRAMMAR
PRÉFÉRER

Préférer is an **-er verb** (just like **aimer, adorer** and **détester** in Unit 5) and it is a **regular** verb. This is how it is conjugated:

Je préfère	*I prefer*	**Nous préférons**	*We prefer*
Tu préfères	*You prefer*	**Vous préférez**	*You (guys) prefer*
Il préfère	*He prefers*	**Ils préfèrent**	*They (m) prefer*
Elle préfère	*She prefers*	**Elles préfèrent**	*They (f) prefer*

9. Match up

Je préfère les bananes	You prefer cheese
Il préfère les tomates	We prefer chocolate
Tu préfères le fromage	They (f) prefer fish
Elles préfèrent le poisson	I prefer bananas
Vous préférez la salade verte	They (m) prefer rice
Nous préférons le chocolat	He prefers tomatoes
Ils préfèrent le riz	You (guys) prefer green salad

10. Slalom translation

Vous préférez	J'adore	Je déteste	Ils préfèrent	Nous aimons	Je n'aime pas
les pommes	les tomates	le lait	la viande	les œufs	les fruits
parce qu'ils	parce que	parce qu'ils	parce qu'elles	parce qu'elles	parce que
sont	sont	sont	sont	c'est	c'est
dégoûtants	malsain	sain	juteuses	délicieux	savoureuses

a. You (guys) prefer meat because it is healthy.

b. I love fruit because they are delicious.

c. I hate eggs because they are disgusting.

d. They prefer apples because they are tasty.

e. We like tomatoes because they are juicy.

f. I don't like milk because it is unhealthy.

11. Translate into English

a. J'aime un peu l'eau...

b. ...parce que c'est sain.

c. Nous préférons le poulet rôti...

d. ...parce que c'est délicieux.

e. Elles n'aiment pas les hamburgers...

f. ...parce qu'ils sont épicés.

g. Vous préférez les pommes...

h. ...parce qu'elles sont sucrées.

12. Spot and correct the errors

a. J'aime la riz parce que c'est savoureux.

b. J'adore les tomates. Ils sont juteuses.

c. Je déteste les chocolats. Ils sont grasses.

d. Je préfère le pain parce que cest sain.

e. Je n'aime pas le chocolate.

f. J'aime un peu la crevettes.

g. Je préfère la viande. Elles sont épicé.

h. Tu aime les bananes?

13. Choose the correct answer

a. J'aime un peu **le fromage** / **la viande** / **les œufs**.   *I like cheese a bit.*

b. Ils sont **délicieux** / **gras** / **sains**.   *They are healthy.*

c. Nous n'aimons pas **le lait** / **le poisson** / **le poulet rôti**.   *We don't like fish.*

d. Vous préférez **les bananes** / **les fraises** / **les oranges**.   *You (guys) prefer strawberries.*

e. C'est **dégoûtant** / **épicé** / **savoureux**.   *It's tasty.*

f. Elles sont **dures** / **grasses** / **juteuses**.   *They are greasy.*

14. Arrange the words in the correct order.

a. le poisson J'aime beaucoup c'est sain parce que.
   I like fish a lot because it is healthy.

b. parce qu'ils sont les hamburgers gras Ils n'aiment pas.
   They don't like burgers because they are greasy.

c. le poulet rôti Vous aimez?
   Do you (guys) like roast chicken?

d. parce qu'elles sont les crevettes Nous préférons délicieuses.
   We prefer prawns because they are delicious.

e. juteuses les oranges Elle déteste parce qu'elles sont.
   She hates oranges because they are juicy.

f. le chocolat parce que J'aime un peu c'est sucré.
   I like chocolate a bit because it is sweet.

15. Tangled translation

a. Je n'aime pas le **milk**. C'est **disgusting**.

b. J'adore **eggs** parce qu'**they are** sains.

c. **He likes** le poulet rôti. **It is** savoureux.

d. Tu aimes les **strawberries** ou les **apples**?

e. **You hate** les tomates. **They are** juteuses.

f. J'adore **chocolates.** Ils sont **delicious.**

g. **We like** les bananes. **They are tasty.**

h. Elles adorent le **honey. It is sweet**.

16. Translate into French

a. I love eggs because they are delicious.

b. We like chocolate because it is sweet.

c. He likes green salad. It is refreshing.

d. You (guys) don't like bread.

e. She likes vegetables. They are healthy.

f. They prefer honey because it is tasty.

g. You don't like meat because it is greasy.

h. I love prawns because they are spicy.

UNIT 14 – ORAL PING PONG – Person A

ENGLISH	FRENCH	ENGLISH	FRENCH
I love chocolate.	J'adore le chocolat.	It's delicious.	C'est délicieux.
You like cheese a lot.		It's tasty.	
I like green salad.	J'aime la salade verte.	It's refreshing.	C'est rafraîchissant.
He likes fish a bit.		It's healthy.	
I don't like burgers.	Je n'aime pas les hamburgers.	They are (m) greasy.	Ils sont gras.
You (guys) hate apples.		They are (f) hard.	
We prefer oranges.	Nous préfèrons les oranges.	They are (f) juicy.	Elles sont juteuses.
They (f) love fruit because they are delicious.		He likes meat because it is tasty.	
I don't like prawns because they are disgusting.	Je n'aime pas les crevettes parce qu'elles sont dégoûtantes.	I hate strawberries because they are sweet.	Je déteste les fraises parce qu'elles sont sucrées.
She doesn't like milk because it is greasy.		He loves roast chicken because it is delicious.	

UNIT 14 – ORAL PING PONG – Person B

ENGLISH	FRENCH	ENGLISH	FRENCH
I love chocolate.		It's delicious.	
You like cheese a lot.	Tu aimes beaucoup le fromage.	It's tasty.	C'est savoureux.
I like green salad.		It's refreshing.	
He likes fish a bit.	Il aime un peu le poisson.	It's healthy.	C'est sain.
I don't like burgers.		They are (m) greasy.	
You (guys) hate apples.	Vous détestez les pommes.	They are (f) hard.	Elles sont dures.
We prefer oranges.		They are (f) juicy.	
They (f) love fruit because they are delicious.	Elles adorent les fruits parce qu'ils sont délicieux.	He likes meat because it is tasty.	Il aime la viande parce que c'est savoureux.
I don't like prawns because they are disgusting.		I hate strawberries because they are sweet.	
She doesn't like milk because it is greasy.	Elle n'aime pas le lait parce que c'est gras.	He loves roast chicken because it is delicious.	Il adore le poulet rôti parce que c'est délicieux.

No Snakes No Ladders

	1	2	3	4	5	6	7
DÉPART	J'adore le café parce que c'est délicieux.	J'aime beaucoup le chocolat parce que c'est sucré.	Nous aimons un peu l'eau parce que c'est sain.	Tu aimes le fromage?	Il déteste le poisson parce que c'est sain.	Tu aimes la salade verte?	Elle adore les fruits parce qu'ils sont sucrés.
15 Elle aime les hamburgers parce qu'ils sont juteux.	**14** J'aime le riz parce que c'est sain.	**13** Tu aimes le jus de fruits?	**12** Nous aimons les oranges parce qu'elles sont juteuses.	**11** J'aime un peu les chocolats parce qu'ils sont sucrés.	**10** Je n'aime pas les pommes parce qu'elles sont dures.	**9** Ils détestent les hamburgers parce qu'ils sont gras.	**8** Je préfère les oranges parce qu'elles sont juteuses.
16 Elle préfère les crevettes parce qu'elles sont saines.	**17** Il aime les crevettes parce qu'elles sont épicées.	**18** Tu aimes les tomates?	**19** Vous préférez les légumes parce qu'ils sont sains.	**20** Je préfère les bananes parce qu'elles sont saines.	**21** Vous aimez le lait?	**22** Elle aime le poulet rôti parce que c'est savoureux.	**23** J'adore les légumes parce qu'ils sont sains.
ARRIVÉE	**30** Tu préfères les oranges ou les pommes?	**29** Vous aimez la salade verte parce que c'est sain.	**28** Tu aimes le pain?	**27** Je n'aime pas les pommes parce qu'elles sont dures.	**26** Il déteste les tomates parce qu'elles sont juteuses.	**25** Ils n'aiment pas les œufs parce qu'ils sont gras.	**24** Tu aimes le miel?

No Snakes No Ladders

START	**1** I love coffee because it is delicious.	**2** I like chocolate a lot because it is sweet.	**3** We like water a bit because it is healthy.	**4** Do you like cheese?	**5** He hates fish because it is healthy.	**6** Do you like green salad?	**7** She loves fruit because they are sweet.
15 She likes hamburgers because they are juicy.	**14** I like rice because it is healthy.	**13** Do you like fruit juice?	**12** We like oranges because they are juicy.	**11** I like chocolates a bit because they are sweet.	**10** I don't like apples because they are hard.	**9** They hate hamburgers because they are greasy.	**8** I prefer oranges because they are juicy.
16 She prefers prawns because they are healthy.	**17** He likes prawns because they are spicy.	**18** Do you like tomatoes?	**19** You (guys) prefer vegetables because they are healthy.	**20** I prefer bananas because they are healthy.	**21** Do you (guys) like milk?	**22** She likes roast chicken because it is tasty.	**23** I love vegetables because they are healthy.
FINISH	**30** Do you prefer oranges or apples?	**29** You (guys) like green salad because it is healthy.	**28** Do you like bread?	**27** I don't like apples because they are hard.	**26** He hates tomatoes because they are juicy.	**25** They (m) don't like eggs because they are greasy.	**24** Do you like honey?

UNIT 14 – FAST & FURIOUS – ROUND 1

1. Bonjour. Qu'est-ce que tu _________ _________ et _________?
   Hello. What do you like to eat and drink?

2. J' _________ _________ le poisson et les _________ parce qu'ils sont _________.
   I like a lot fish and vegetables because they are delicious.

3. Je n'aime pas les _________ parce qu'_____ _____ épicées.
   I don't like prawns because they are spicy.

4. Mon frère _________ _________ _________ parce qu'ils sont _________.
   My brother likes eggs because they are tasty.

5. Ma meilleure amie _________ le _________ parce que _________ _________.
   My best friend prefers chocolate because it is sweet.

	Time 1	Time 2	Time 3	Time 4
Time				
Mistakes				

UNIT 14 – FAST & FURIOUS – ROUND 2

1. Bonjour. Qu'est-ce que tu _________ _________ et _________?
   Hello. What do you like to eat and drink?

2. J' _________ _________ le pain et les _________ parce qu'ils sont _________.
   I like bread a lot and fruit because they are tasty.

3. Je n'aime pas les _________ parce qu'_____ _____ juteuses.
   I don't like strawberries because they are juicy.

4. Mon frère _________ _________ _________ parce qu'ils sont _________.
   My brother likes chocolates because they are sweet.

5. Ma meilleure amie _________ le _________ parce que _________ _________.
   My best friend prefers milk because it is refreshing.

	Time 1	Time 2	Time 3	Time 4
Time				
Mistakes				

ASSESSMENT ROUND

1. Choose the correct translation (you won't need two of the sentences)

a. Tu préfères le fromage ou le chocolat?   _____

b. J'adore le poisson parce que c'est sain et délicieux.   _____

c. Je n'aime pas les hamburgers parce qu'ils sont gras.   _____

d. Il aime les pommes parce qu'elles sont dures.   _____

e. Il adore les fraises parce qu'elles sont juteuses.   _____

1. I love fish because it is tasty and delicious.
2. I love fish because it is healthy and delicious.
3. He likes apples because they are hard.
4. He loves strawberries because they are juicy.
5. Do you prefer cheese or chocolate?
6. I don't like burgers because they are greasy.
7. He loves strawberries because they are sweet.

2. Fill in the gaps with the missing words

a. Il préfère les __________ parce qu'elles sont délicieuses.

b. Elle déteste les oranges parce qu'elles sont __________.

c. J'aime un peu le chocolat parce que __________ sucré.

d. J'adore les légumes parce qu'____ ______ savoureux.

e. Je __________ les pommes parce qu'elles sont dégoûtantes.

sucrées	ils sont	bananes	c'est	déteste

3. Translate the sentences into French

a. We hate tomatoes because they are disgusting.

b. You (guys) like chicken a lot because it is healthy.

c. He hates fish because it is greasy.

d. Do you (guys) prefer fish or meat?

e. They (f) don't like fruit juice because it is sweet.

UNIT 15
My holiday plans
(Talking about future plans for holidays)

Main grammar focus:

- Review of the immediate future

Pop-up grammar:

- To use the conditional

UNIT 15
My holiday plans

Où vas-tu aller cet été?	*Where are you going to go this summer?*
Comment vas-tu voyager?	*How are you going to travel?*
Combien de temps vas-tu passer là-bas?	*How long are you going to spend over there?*
Où vas-tu rester?	*Where are you going to stay?*
Que vas-tu faire pendant les vacances?	*What are you going to do during the holidays?*

Cet été, je vais aller en vacances en *This summer I am going to go on holiday to* **Nous allons aller en** *We are going to go to*	Allemagne Angleterre Bourgogne Bretagne Espagne	**en avion** *by plane* **en bateau** *by boat* **en car** *by coach* **en voiture** *by car*	
Je vais passer… *I am going to spend* **Nous allons passer…** *We are going to spend*	**une semaine** *1 week* **deux semaines** *2 weeks*	**là-bas** *over there* **avec ma famille** *with my family*	**Ce sera ennuyeux** *It will be boring* **Ce sera amusant** *It will be fun* **Ce sera génial** *It will be great*
Je vais rester dans *I am going to stay in* **Nous allons rester dans** *We are going to stay in*	la maison de ma famille **un camping** **un hôtel bon marché** *a cheap hotel* **un hôtel de luxe** *a luxury hotel*		
Je vais… *I am going to…* **Nous allons…** *We are going to…* **J'aimerais…** **Je voudrais…** *I would like to…* **Nous aimerions…** **Nous voudrions…** *We would like to…*	**acheter des souvenirs** *buy souvenirs* **aller à la plage** *go to the beach* **aller en boîte** *go clubbing* **bronzer** *sunbathe* **danser** *dance* **faire des courses** *go shopping* **faire de la plongée** *go scuba diving* **faire du sport** *do sport* **faire du tourisme** *go sightseeing* **faire du vélo** *go biking* **jouer avec des amis** *play with some friends* **jouer de la guitare** *play the guitar* **manger et dormir** *eat and sleep* **manger de la nourriture délicieuse** *eat delicious food* **me/nous reposer** *rest* **sortir en ville** *go out into town*		

MAIN GRAMMAR FOCUS
THE IMMEDIATE FUTURE

The immediate future is used to express what you are going to do in the near future.

Example: **Je <u>vais</u> passer une semaine là-bas.**

I <u>am going</u> to spend one week over there.

To form the immediate future, you need to use the verb **aller** in the present tense and the infinitive afterwards, just like in the grid below:

Je	*I*	**vais**	*am going*		
Tu	*You*	**vas**	*are going*		
Il/Elle	*He/She*	**va**	*is going*	**aller**	*to go*
Nous	*We*	**allons**	*are going*	**acheter**	*to buy*
Vous	*You (guys)*	**allez**	*are going*	**faire**	*to do*
Ils/Elles	*They*	**vont**	*are going*	**jouer**	*to play*

Nous <u>allons</u> faire de la plongée.
We <u>are going</u> to go scuba diving.

---

1. Match up

Je vais aller	They (f) are going to do
Tu vas passer	I am going to go
Ils vont rester	We are going to go out
Elles vont faire	He is going to eat
Vous allez jouer	You are going to spend
Il va manger	You (guys) are going to play
Nous allons sortir	They going to stay

2. Complete with the missing letters

a. J _ v _ _ s _ ll _ r au parc.
  I am going to go to the park.

b. _ ls v _ _ t d _ ns _ r.
  They are going to dance.

c. T _ v _ s f _ _ r _ du sport.
  You are going to do sport.

d. _ ll _ v _ br _ nz _ r.
  She is going to sunbathe.

3. Complete with the missing verbs in the immediate future

a. Cet été je _____________ aller en Bretagne.

This summer, I am going to go to Brittany.

b. Nous _____________ passer deux semaines là-bas.

We are going to spend two weeks there.

c. Tu _____________ rester dans un camping.

You are going to stay on a campsite.

d. Elle _____________ faire des courses.

She is going to go shopping.

e. Vous _____________ manger et dormir.

You (guys) are going to eat and sleep.

f. Ils _____________ faire du vélo.

They are going to go biking.

g. Elles _____________ bronzer.

They are going to sunbathe.

h. Nous _____________ sortir en ville.

We are going to go out into town.

---

4. Break the flow

a. JevaisallerenBourgogneenvoiture.

b. Ilvaacheterdessouvenirs.

c. Ellesvontfairedutourisme.

d. Tuvasjoueravecdesamis.

e. Vousallezmangeretdormir.

f. Nousallonsfairedelaplongée.

g. Ilsvontallerenboîte.

h. Nousallonsfairedusport.

5. Faulty translation: fix the English

a. Je vais aller en Angleterre.
I would like to go to England.

b. Nous allons rester dans un hôtel.
You are going to stay in a hotel.

c. Elle va faire du vélo.
She is going to go sightseeing.

d. Ils vont aller à la plage.
He is going to go to the beach.

e. Vous allez jouer avec des amis.
You (guys) are going to talk to some friends.

---

6. Choose the correct verb

a. Je **vais / vas** aller en France.

b. Tu **vas / va** rester dans un camping.

c. Ils **vont / va** aller à la plage.

d. Nous **allons / allez** faire du tourisme.

e. Elles **va / vont** se reposer.

f. Vous **allez / allons** jouer de la guitare.

g. Elle **va / vas** sortir en ville.

h. Nous **va / allons** bronzer.

7. Translate into French

a. I am going to dance.

b. We are going to rest.

c. You are going to go scuba diving.

d. She is going to eat and sleep.

e. We are going to stay in a hotel.

f. They (f) are going to go biking.

g. You (guys) are going to go shopping.

h. They (m) are going to do sport.

POP UP GRAMMAR
THE CONDITIONAL

The CONDITIONAL is used to express what you would do or would like to do.

Example: **Je voudrais aller au parc cet après-midi.**
I would like to go to the park this afternoon.

Here is how to form the conditional of **vouloir** and **aimer:**

Je voudrais **J'aimerais**	*I would like*	**aller** **acheter** **faire**	*to go* *to buy* *to do*
Il / Elle voudrait **Il / Elle aimerait**	*He / She would like*	**jouer** **manger**	*to play* *to eat*

Elle aimerait faire du sport.
She would like to do sport.

---

8. Match up

Je voudrais manger.	She would like to do.
Il aimerait jouer.	He would like to spend.
Elle aimerait faire.	I would like to buy.
Elle voudrait aller.	I would like to eat.
J'aimerais acheter.	She would like to go.
Il voudrait passer.	He would like to play.

9. Complete with the missing letters

a. J _ v _ _ dr _ _ s _ ll _ r en boîte.
   I would like to go clubbing.

b. _ l v _ _ dr _ _ t j _ _ er avec des amis.
   He would like to play with some friends.

c. J' _ _ m _ r _ _ _ m _ _ g _ _.
   I would like to eat.

d. _ ll _ v _ _ dr _ _ _ br _ nz _ r.
   She would like to sunbathe.

---

10. Complete with the missing verbs in the conditional

a. Cet été je ______________ aller en Bretagne.   *This summer, I would like to go to Brittany.*

b. Elle ______________ passer deux semaines là-bas.   *She would like to spend two weeks there.*

c. Il ______________ rester dans un camping.   *He would like to stay on a campsite.*

d. Je ______________ faire des courses.   *I would like to go shopping.*

e. Je ______________ manger et dormir.   *I would like to eat and sleep.*

f. Il ______________ faire du vélo.   *He would like to go biking.*

g. Elle ______________ bronzer.   *She would like to sunbathe.*

h. J' ______________ sortir en ville.   *I would like to go out into town.*

11. Slalom translation

Cet été	Vous allez	Nous allons	Je voudrais	Ma mère	Mon père
voudrait	faire du	je vais aller	rester dans	va	voyager en
avion et	faire des	un camping	faire du sport	en vacances	tourisme
courses et	en France	et faire du	aussi en	et faire de	et aussi dans
un hôtel	vélo	la plongée	avec ma famille	danser	voiture

a. This summer, I am going to go on holiday to France with my family.

b. You (guys) are going to travel by plane and also by car.

c. We are going to stay on a campsite and also in a hotel.

d. I would like to go sightseeing and go biking.

e. My mother would like to do sport and go scuba diving.

f. My father is going to go shopping and dance.

12. Translate into English

a. Je vais rester dans un camping bon marché.

b. Nous allons passer une semaine là-bas.

c. Il va rester dans un hôtel bon marché.

d. J'aimerais jouer avec des amis.

e. Je voudrais rester dans un hôtel de luxe.

f. Il voudrait rester avec ma famille.

g. Vous allez aller en boîte.

h. J'aimerais me reposer.

13. Spot and correct the errors

a. Je vas aller en Allemagne.

b. Tu vas passes une semaine là-bas.

c. Je aimerais rester dans un hôtel de luxe.

d. Nous allions faire de la plongée.

e. Il vas jouer de la guitare.

f. Elle faire du tourisme.

g. Il voudrais rester dans un hôtel.

h. Je voudrais j'achète des souvenirs.

14. Choose the correct answer

a. Je vais aller **à la plage / à la piscine / en boîte**. *I'm going to go to the pool.*

b. Il voudrait **bronzer / danser / sortir en ville**. *He would like to go out into town.*

c. Ils vont faire **des courses / de la plongée / du sport**. *They are going to go shopping.*

d. Elle aimerait **dormir / se reposer / faire du vélo**. *She would like to go biking.*

e. Nous allons **nous reposer / faire du sport / bronzer**. *We're going to sunbathe.*

f. Elle va faire **du sport / du tourisme / du vélo**. *She is going to go sightseeing.*

a. en vacances en bateau Je vais aller en Angleterre.
   I am going to go on holiday to England by boat.

b. avec ma famille une semaine Nous allons passer.
   We are going to spend one week with my family.

c. elles vont manger du tourisme et Elles vont faire de la nourriture délicieuse.
   They are going to go sightseeing and they are going to eat delicious food.

d. va faire des souvenirs et Mon père ma mère du vélo va acheter.
   My father is going to go biking and my mother is going to buy souvenirs.

e. Mon frère se reposer voudrait et en ville ma sœur sortir aimerait.
   My brother would like to rest and my sister would like to go out into town.

16. Choose the correct translation

a.	**I am going to stay**	je vais aller	je vais rester	je vais faire
b.	**You (guys) are going to eat**	vous allez manger	vous allez boire	vous allez aller
c.	**She is going to go**	elle va partir	elle va sortir	elle va aller
d.	**I would like to go**	je voudrais aller	je voudrais sortir	je voudrais faire
e.	**We are going to do**	nous allons aller	nous allons faire	nous allons sortir
f.	**He would like to do**	il voudrait rester	il voudrait faire	il voudrait aller
g.	**I would like to sleep**	j'aimerais manger	j'aimerais dormir	j'aimerais boire
h.	**He would like to dance**	il aimerait danser	il aimerait jouer	il aimerait aller

17. Guided translation: complete the translation

a. *I am going to go clubbing and dance.*   Je _____ ______ en boîte et je _____ ______ .

b. *Where are you (guys) going to go on hols?*   Où _______-vous ______ en vacances?

c. *We are going to stay in a luxury hotel.*   Nous _______ ________ dans un hôtel de luxe.

d. *He is going to eat food.*   Il ____ ___________ de la nourriture.

e. *I would like to go shopping.*   J'_________ faire les ____________ .

f. *She would like to stay in a campsite.*   Elle _________ _______ dans un camping.

18. Tangled translation

a. Je vais **to spend** une semaine en **England**.

b. **You are going to** rester **in the** maison de ma **family**.

c. **I would like** faire du sport.

d. Où **are you going to go** cet été?

e. Comment allez **you (guys)** voyager?

f. **We are going to go out** en ville.

g. **She would like** aller en boîte.

h. Il **would like** manger du poulet.

19. Translate into French

a. This summer I am going to go to Spain.

b. You (guys) are going to travel by plane.

c. I would like to stay in a luxury hotel.

d. He would like to do sport.

e. We are going to rest.

f. Where are you going to stay?

g. My mother would like to sunbathe.

h. They (m) are going to play the guitar.

No Snakes No Ladders

DÉPART	**1** Où vas-tu aller cet été?	**2** Il va aller en boîte.	**3** Je vais rester dans un camping.	**4** Cet été, je vais aller en Allemagne.	**5** Je voudrais danser.	**6** Elle aimerait faire du vélo.	**7** Vous allez passer une semaine là-bas.
15 Vous allez rester dans un camping.	**14** Je vais me reposer.	**13** Comment vas-tu voyager?	**12** Je vais manger et dormir.	**11** Elle aimerait jouer de la guitare.	**10** Elle va bronzer.	**9** Nous allons aller en Bretagne.	**8** Il aimerait jouer avec des amis.
16 Tu vas aller à la plage.	**17** J'aimerais faire du tourisme.	**18** Nous allons rester dans un hôtel bon marché.	**19** Elles vont sortir en ville.	**20** Combien de temps vas-tu passer là-bas?	**21** Il voudrait faire des courses.	**22** Ils vont passer deux semaines là-bas.	**23** Il voudrait faire de la plongée.
ARRIVÉE	**30** Je vais acheter des souvenirs.	**29** Elle voudrait faire du sport.	**28** Qu'est-ce que tu vas faire?	**27** Elle aimerait voyager en car.	**26** Il va voyager en avion.	**25** Il voudrait manger et dormir.	**24** Où vas-tu rester?

No Snakes No Ladders

START	**1** Where are you going to go this summer?	**2** He is going to go clubbing.	**3** I am going to stay on a campsite.	**4** This summer I am going to go to Germany.	**5** I would like to dance.	**6** She would like to go biking.	**7** You (guys) are going to spend a week there.
15 You (guys) are going to stay on a campsite.	**14** I am going to rest.	**13** How are you going to travel?	**12** I am going to eat and sleep.	**11** She would like to play the guitar.	**10** She is going to sunbathe.	**9** We are going to go to Britany.	**8** He would like to play with his friends.
16 You are going to go to the beach.	**17** I would like to go sightseeing.	**18** We are going to stay in a cheap hotel.	**19** They (f) are going to go out into town.	**20** How long are you going to spend over there?	**21** He would like to go shopping.	**22** They (m) are going to spend two weeks there.	**23** He would like to go scuba diving.
FINISH	**30** I am going to buy souvenirs.	**29** She would like to do sport.	**28** What are you going to do?	**27** She would like to travel by coach.	**26** He is going to travel by plane.	**25** He would like to eat and sleep.	**24** Where are you going to stay?

UNIT 15 – FAST & FURIOUS – ROUND 1

1. Bonjour. Où _____-tu _________ cet été?
   Hello. Where are you going to go this summer?

2. Je ______ ________ en Allemagne en _________.
   I am going to go to Germany by plane.

3. Je ______ ________ une semaine avec ____ __________.
   I am going to spend a week with my family.

4. Nous _______ _________ dans la __________ de ma famille.
   We are going to stay in the family home.

5. Je ___________ ________ du tourisme et ________ des __________.
   I would like to go sighseeing and go shopping.

	Time 1	Time 2	Time 3	Time 4
Time				
Mistakes				

UNIT 15 – FAST & FURIOUS – ROUND 2

1. Bonjour. Où _____-tu _________ cet été?
   Hello. Where are you going to go this summer?

2. Je ______ ________ en Espagne en _________.
   I am going to go to Spain by car.

3. Je ______ ________ deux semaines ____-______.
   I am going to spend two weeks there.

4. Nous _______ _________ dans un hôtel ____ _______.
   We are going to stay in a luxury hotel.

5. J' ___________ ________ du vélo et ________ avec des __________.
   I would like to go biking and play with some friends.

	Time 1	Time 2	Time 3	Time 4
Time				
Mistakes				

ASSESSMENT ROUND

1. Choose the correct translation (you won't need two of the sentences)

a. Qu'est-ce que tu vas faire pendant les vacances?   _____

b. Nous allons manger et dormir et faire du tourisme.   _____

c. Je vais rester dans un hôtel bon marché.   _____

d. Mon père voudrait passer une semaine en Bourgogne.   _____

e. Je voudrais rester dans la maison de ma famille.   _____

   1.   I would like to stay in the family home.
   2.   We are going to eat and sleep and go sightseeing.
   3.   I would like to stay in a big house.
   4.   My father would like to spend a week in Bourgogne.
   5.   What are you going to do during the holidays?
   6.   I am going to stay in a cheap hotel.
   7.   We are going to eat and sleep and go scuba diving.

2. Fill in the gaps with the missing words

a. Où vas-tu _________ cet été?

b. Je _________ aller en vacances en Espagne en avion.

c. Combien de temps _________-tu passer là-bas?

d. Je vais _________ une semaine avec ma famille.

e. Je voudrais _________ des souvenirs et bronzer sur la plage.

vas	aller	acheter	passer	vais

3. Translate the sentences into French

a. This summer, I am going to go on holiday to Spain with my family.

b. You (guys) are going to travel by boat and also by car.

c. We are going to stay in a cheap hotel.

d. They (m) are going to go sightseeing and they (f) are going to go scuba diving.

e. My mother would like to go biking and go shopping.

The End

We hope you have enjoyed using this GRAMMAR BOOK and found it useful!

As many of you will appreciate, the penguin is a fantastic animal. At Language Gym, we hold it as a symbol of resilience, bravery and good humour; able to thrive in the harshest possible environments, and with, arguably the best gait in the animal kingdom (black panther or penguin, you choose). You too will need resilience and good-humour in your quest to master French grammar! Bon courage!

The Language Gym Team